"HOOD ESTATE"

THE MANUAL

By Leonard Person Jr.

LEONARD "SPAR" PERSON JR.

Novel Written By: Leonard "Spar" Person Jr.

Novel Transcribed By: CO. Isadore Johnson

Novel Published By: Hood Estate LLC

ISBN# 978-0-9799904-0-3

Printed in the U.S.A.

Copyright: 2007

Editor: Rachel Lewis

Published: 2007

Graphics By: AR-C Designs

LEONARD "SPAR" PERSON JR.

This book is dedicated to my little cousin **Tavian Gaines** who died battling his fight with cancer in September of 2007. He was only 6 years old (We all miss and Love you little man. RIP) To the strongest mother on the planet, my Aunt **Venisha Gaines**, keep your head up Aunty, you've done a wonderful job. **Love You.**

Phenomenal Thank You To

My **Lord and Savior Jesus Christ** without you Life isn't possible. Thank You so much for rewarding me by blessing me and answering my prayers for my hard earned work. I will forever serve you with my heart, flesh and soul. Thank You!

Special Thank You To

My Daughter **Heaven Ivy Lewis Person** you gave me the motivation, determination, inspiration and sacrifice to succeed. You are definitely a blessing from God. I

LEONARD "SPAR" PERSON JR.

love you forever sweetie and you will always be **DA DA BABY**.

Thank You to

Valarie Person (Mom), Leonard Person SR (Father), Ellease Ward (great grandma), Tiffany Person (sister), Christopher Person (brother), Christina Person (sister), Rachel Lewis Person (Wife), Octavia Lewis, Nasir Martinez, Kevin Person, Gary Stewart, Isadore Johnson, Khalis and David Ward, Myron and Ronnie, DJ Evil Dee and Family, Butta L, Vernal Shaw, Ravin Jagoo, Adonis Hill, Brenda Person, Johnny Brown, Abraham Hoschander , Kathy Denington, Kester D., Brian Person, Chaka Virgil, Nazaam Shinn, Tanzia James, Deetrek Davis, Enoch and David Forbin, Gerod Huggins, Ramel Davis, Anthony Russin, Everton Young Rico, Donald Edge and Family, Vincent Gaines, Dee Dee and Ellis, Taron McCleod, Shamika-Javon and Larry Gaines,

LEONARD "SPAR" PERSON JR.

Khalif Gaines, Alan Person, Grandma Person, Uncle Tyrone, Jack Mann and Mark From Valley Funding, Ben Frankle, Raymond and Alicia From Capital Homes, Cash Flow Funding, ASAP Appraisal, Money Making Moves, Cash and Ryan, Pat-Charles-Derrick and Chris from Imperial aka Axiom, Diamond Title, Roger Crawford, Jamel George, Infenie Fortune,

LEONARD "SPAR" PERSON JR.

Contents

Introduction

LEONARD "SPAR" PERSON JR.

From Bushwick, Brooklyn, NY introducing SPAR. Here's a brief description of this business savvy young man on the rise:

SPAR is definitely a Jack of all trades. But before he got into all the entrepreneurial ventures, Hip hop or rather Street Music was his first love. He was inspired by a lot of MC's such as Nas, Biggie, Tupac, Jay-z, LL Cool-J, Krs1, Ice Cube, Busta, Rakim, Kool G Rap, Redman, Method Man.

The closest he got to taste the fame was being under the wing of Black Moon, break dancing and trying to freestyle at local parties with the founding members. When the group finally made it SPAR knew that he could make it too because he had been around and saw how they came from nothing and made it. He started rhyming at the age of 12 years old when his cousin Dave taught him how to flow. He shortly realized he had a knack for words, a way with sound and talent that could move a crowd. Making his way with several other rhymesters he formed several groups that would never rise to become anything but hood celebs. Not too long after he hooked up with Freedom, who was the leading act of music group C & C Music Factory. He would go on to sign a management deal with Freedom and travel on tour with him as well. Although the experience was great, it never sparked anything big for him; Soon after he found himself back on a musical grind. Every year he tried to get noticed by record labels but nobody responded with a good deal. He never stopped improving his craft but it wasn't helping him get anywhere. So he went back to his books in hopes of combining book knowledge with some street smarts. After graduating from Maxwell Vocational High in "98, SPAR formed Money Making Moves Entertainment the label. He followed that with what was soon to become the DDF Crew. On his right hand was his closest friend and current business partner Twin. He attempted again to make a name for himself performing at different venues, as it goes in the game no one saw his genius. Again the game and his dreams took a back seat to real life. He got a job at Marriott Hotel in Manhattan for the next 5 years in hopes of keeping together a family that was slowly falling apart and maybe getting his money up to do it all his way. He wasn't going to wait on the support of a big label. He had ideas and a hunger not easily suppressed. While he was working crazy hours washing dishes, mopping and sweeping at the hotel his family problems were getting worse. At home his mother and father were breaking up and the house in Bushwick was being auction off. Everybody was out on the street, having to deal with the NYC shelter system and a slew of other problems plaguing the homeless. With his parents' finances in disarray and their main focus being on the younger siblings, he was living on the edge and sleeping anywhere he could. SPAR kept his head up and prayed for the Lord's help. SPAR kept his faith even after being fired from the Marriott. He did what most black men in his day and age tend to do, he took to the streets. His family depended on him and so his grind became relentless. He started selling clothes, CDs, DVDs, weed and a bunch of other shit; courtesy of several childhood friends also in similar situations. To top it all off he was collecting an unemployment check. Already building a life with his girl and a child, he soon found out he had another one on the way. With another mouth to feed he realized that a life behind bars was not an option. Too many people counted on him.

A change of fate.

Through the many people he had come in contact with he met a man that would soon become the answer to his prayers. SPAR met his inspiration and current business partner Ravin aka Mr. Money Bags, a mortgage consultant. He was the same age as SPAR but had at least 5 cribs and 250k in his bank account. From there SPAR and his Mother started working as sales agents at an investment company owned by two brothers. They gave SPAR the opportunity and the foundation for what would soon become a money making empire. Along the way SPAR has met and worked for countless people who would give him the seeds he would need to make a way of his own (which he had planned on doing one way or another). SPAR worked on commission and in 3 months he made 60k for himself and 1.5 million for the company. He became the most unlikely employee coming to work in his jeans and timbs, yet the most dedicated employee in this small company. With his way with words and the confidence he gained from countless rhyme battles SPAR knew that he couldn't fail. He now had all the things he needed to start his own business. SPAR resigned and opened up his own investment company Heaven Homes LLC., named after his new baby girl. He started flipping property and hired every hustler he knew to come and work for him. Hence Hood Estate was born. He taught a lot of young dudes the game and how they could generate income for the movement taking place, but also for themselves; Because at the end of the day everyone wants to be their own boss.

SPAR now owns Money Making Moves Ent., Heaven Homes LLC, Hood Estate LLC, Tipsi Liquors LLC and countless other investment ventures that include, credit repair, construction, interior design, clothes, movies and books. Though his many ventures keep him busy he has enough people on his team to return to his first love. The Rap Game. And he has all the money he needs to finally do it all his way!

LEONARD "SPAR" PERSON JR.

Chapter One

"Establishing Credit/Repair"

"When it comes to being successful in life there are many different roads to travel down to arrive at that destination. One thing is for sure, whichever road you do decide to take, there is no shortcut. To all my dudes out there in the game and on the grind, we all know no matter how good it treats us in the beginning, we also know where that shortcut leads us sooner or later... I have found these phrases to be perhaps two of the truest of all statements I've ever heard mentioned. The reason being is that in order to realistically achieve important goals or obtain noteworthy things in life, certain requirements are just absolutely necessary. In the world of real estate, I've found the same as being true. There is nothing more critical and straight forward when dealing with real estate than the issue of credit. Without it, you don't even exist to banks, **creditors** or any of the other essential entities that hold the critical keys to finance countless real estate opportunities. The only way around this chapter is if you're already rich and don't need the assistance of loans from an outside source. Even then, **credit** is important because who wants to put up their own cash when you don't have to.

In this chapter, I have broken down all the basics in order to begin your journey to establishing sufficient credit. This will also include how to repair credit that has been damaged.

? What is a credit bureau?

Credit bureaus are also known as credit reporting agencies. Credit reporting agencies are the gatekeepers of consumer credit information and are major players in what we refer to as the "credit cycle."

A credit agency is an entity that assembles consumer credit information and other information on consumers for the purpose of "selling" the information (in the form of a **credit report**) to third party subscribers.

While there are over 2,000 credit reporting agencies in the United States, three giants dominate the industry" Experian, TransUnion and Equifax. They are big and they are powerful. They maintain some 750 million credit files on over 200 million Americans. They are also intimidating! With the advent of the computer, the credit bureaus have become powerful private investigators into your financial life. Whether you like it or not, they are tracking your every financial move.

Most of the banks rely on these credit bureaus to determine if you are a credit worthy individual. You should do everything in your power to make sure that your information in your credit report is correct. Most institutions such as banks, credit card issuers, department stores, car dealers, etc., report to these bureaus regarding the way you pay your **debts**. If you are late it is recorded, together with how much you owe.

Hood Estate can help you challenge and dispute the incorrect information and have items deleted from your report.

Also keep in mind that no one may have access to your credit information without your written permission.

1) <u>Establishing Credit</u>

Almost everyday someone seeks to purchase something only to find that from a cash point of view they just can't afford it straight up. Some people spend countless weeks, months, even years trying to save up from their earnings to buy whatever it is they have their hearts set on. The method nowadays to get around all that is through the use of personal credit.

For the person who has never had **credit**, they can begin by applying for a credit card from a bank in which they have established an account. You can also apply directly to a credit card company such as Visa, MasterCard, etc. Being that the credit lender doesn't have any way of determining whether or not to grant you credit, you will most likely be required to leave a deposit in the amount that the credit card will be issued for. This is called a **secure credit line**. As you use this card to make purchases and pay your monthly bills on time, you will build a credit history and eventually the use of leaving a deposit will no longer be needed.

LEONARD "SPAR" PERSON JR.

Why is credit denied?

The most common reasons for rejection falls into the last two categories: Poor Payment History and Errors in the Credit File. While little can actually be done to remove accurate late payment data from your credit file, information can be challenged, deleted or modified through the techniques created by Hood Estate.

Remember, your credit report is not only the first impression of your credit worthiness; it's the only impression that you leave. As credit consumers, we must arm ourselves with the best weapons possible: knowledge and information.

Hood Estate is pleased to have the opportunity to help you gain a new understanding of the consumer credit system and help you raise your credit scores so you can be approved for a loan from Hood Estate.

LEONARD "SPAR" PERSON JR.

Get Credit Worthy again with Hood Estate.

There are nearly 60,000,000, (that's 60 million) Americans with mediocre credit or bad credit (known in credit reporting as "negative or derogatory" credit).

Many of them are not even aware they have poor credit, having never seen their credit reports. Some with bad credit are not aware that there's anything wrong with their credit because their credit reports contain someone else's **derogatory** information but again, may be unaware that their "good names" have been ruined through no fault of their own.

Most people with bad credit are not aware that they can do something to restore their credit and raise their credit scores. And still others may have given up hope of owning a major credit card because they perceive they are too far down the road of bad credit habits to correct their situation.

LEONARD "SPAR" PERSON JR.

Fortunately, Hood Estate can help.

How do you protect your Credit Status?

The law provides for two reasons to contest an entry on your credit report: "not mine" and "not accurate." "Not mine" is fairly self-explanatory. A listing that is "not accurate" may include (but not limited to) the following:

a) Closed accounts listed as "open"

b) Information, which is outdated (more that 7 years old)

c) Data entry errors (i.e., a "$7.00" overdue remark listed as "$700.00)

d) Incorrect payment information

e) Bills that you have legally refused (i.e., merchandise you returned to a store for credit which is listed as unpaid)

f) Lack of current personal information (address, marital status, job, etc.)

LEONARD "SPAR" PERSON JR.

? Why are so many people spending so much money to repair their damaged credit?

It's simple. If you have bad credit, try buying a car, jewelry, a home, getting a school or cash loan, or even try to open a bank account. Now compound the nightmare if you know that your credit is good but the credit reporting agencies are telling the loan officers that you have a bad record. And if this isn't bad enough, the average American is completely intimidated and uneducated as to their rights and abilities to overcome the Credit Monster. Let's face it; "The Big 3" credit reporting agencies seem to have all the power over your current life as well as your future. It is time to become EDUCATED and EMPOWERED! With KNOWLEDGE, you can and will become determined, committed and organized.

LEONARD "SPAR" PERSON JR.

With Hood Estate, you can succeed!

Hood Estate will help you legally remove any inaccurate or misleading information from your credit files as quickly as possible. We can also help remove other derogatory items through "technicalities,", again using only legal methods. Hood Estate becomes your "secret weapon" to repair your credit and qualify you for the home you deserve.

Furthermore, your credit file may vary from credit reporting agency to agency. All creditors do not subscribe to every bureau, which means that they do not report their information to every bureau. And, the credit reporting agencies do not share information with each other, including the good information that one would want all potential creditors to see.

LEONARD "SPAR" PERSON JR.

Most credit reports include the following general categories of information:

a) Biographical Information

Your full name, current address, previous addresses (especially if you've been at your current address less than two years), social Security Number, Date of Birth, and Place of Employment, if known. It is important to note that self-employed persons are often listed as unemployed on their credit reports. If you are self-employed, be sure to check your credit report for this error and contact the credit reporting agency for immediate correction.

b) ACCOUNT INFORMATION

Name of the creditor/issuer

LEONARD "SPAR" PERSON JR.

DATE ACCOUNT WAS OPENED

Original balance or limit

Current balance

TERMS OF THE ACCOUNT

CURRENT STATUS

c) PUBLIC INFORMATION

Marriages, Divorces, Judgments, Tax Liens, Arrests, Convictions, or Lawsuits against you. Public Records information as contained in this section is usually maintained in the office of the County Clerk.

d) INQUIRIES

An **inquiry** is listed on your credit report each time a creditor or potential creditor requests a copy of your credit report. While this activity is not negative activity, it is often viewed as a "ding" against you, especially if there are inquiries and no new accounts were subsequently opened. In this case, other potential creditors may assume you are piling on new credit and, therefore, new financial obligations.

ACCESS TO YOUR CREDIT FILES

Who, in addition to yourself, has the right to obtain your credit report? **The Fair Credit Reporting Act** established the specific circumstances in which your report can be released. These are:

- By court order
- Upon Request by the consumer
- When the Intended Use is for:

LEONARD "SPAR" PERSON JR.

+ Credit transactions initiated by the consumer

+ Employment purposes

+ Applications for insurance

+ Licenses or other benefits granted by governmental instrumentalities

+ Other legitimate business needs

Credit reports are not always easy to understand. Upon reviewing your own, be prepared to spend the time this exercise deserves. Understanding your credit report is an important first key step to the dispute process. Hood Estate will walk you through the process.

DON'T BE INTIMIDATED. Hood Estate CAN HELP!

Negative information in credit files, including,

anything from late payments to bankruptcy, becomes obsolete after a certain period of time and must be removed from your credit files. By law, credit-reporting agencies must maintain a reporting process that protects the consumer from having obsolete information contained in their credit reports. Section 605 of the Fair Credit Reporting Act sets forth something akin to a statute of limitations for credit offenses and other offenses.

EX: let's suppose one of your accounts were turned over for collection eight years ago. That information is now irrelevant to your credit profile. Under the Fair Credit Reporting Act, this outdated information must be removed from your reports.

2) Disputing Negative Accounts

In the course of utilizing your newly obtained credit

cards it will be your complete responsibility to ensure that you do not abuse your privileges in any form or fashion. Always stay within your means to pay. Turning credit into unaffordable debt is defeating your whole purpose for obtaining credit in the first place. Now despite all that I have just mentioned, there have been situations where a creditor(s) will make a claim stating you made a late payment or in some instances even failed on a payment. Most of the time creditor's claims turn out to be accurate as a result of people's irresponsibility in managing their finances. There are times though where the creditors do make mistakes and report errors. In those instances, it's your duty to confront these claims in formal manner (writing/online) to one or perhaps all three of the governing credit bureaus; Experian, TransUnion, Equifax. There, you can move to rectify your credit history and move forward.

As a consumer, you have the right to dispute any

inaccuracies contained in your credit files. The Fair Credit Reporting Act mandates that the credit-reporting agency must reinvestigate any item of information disputed by you.

EX: when disputing your derogatory accounts you must do so online at one of the credit agency sites. You can also dispute it in writing by providing factual proof clearing you of the negative account. Once the matter is clarified, it's optional to ask for a **credit delete letter** and **settlement letter**. The credit-reporting agency must respond in a reasonable time period and must record the current/corrected status of that information. By law, the credit-reporting agency must do as above, unless there are reasonable grounds to believe that your request is "frivolous" or "irrelevant."

Hood Estate provides a comprehensive system so that you can chart your course of action and keep track of your progress.

3) <u>Building Trade Lines</u>

Another way of establishing credit is through the use of a method called "piggyback riding" or OPC (Other People's Credit). This means that you will seek to establish credit by becoming an **authorized borrower** on someone else's credit account. Because your social security number is added onto the account, the credit bureaus will receive monthly reports on your purchase/payment activity. This along with the fact that the person who has put you on their account will already have substantially good credit; you in turn will receive a significant boost in your credit rating.

Another way of establishing credit is by becoming a **Joint Account Holder** on someone else's credit account.

LEONARD "SPAR" PERSON JR.

There is a difference between being a Joint Account Holder verses an Authorized Borrower. Authorized Borrower accounts show up on your credit report as just that, authorized borrower (AB). When you're a Joint Account Holder, your account will show up as a primary account (meaning, it will appear that you are the owner of the account).

The disadvantage of making someone a Joint Account Holder is that they have access to your account. A Joint Account Holder can make changes to your account just as you would do. Also, if you want to remove someone from your account, you would have to appear with that Joint Account Holder in person in order for them to sign their name off of your account. In other cases, the credit card company will send you a form that requires both the Joint Account Holder's and the primary account holder's (YOU) signature. If for some reason the Joint Account Holder decides they don't want to sign any papers to remove their name from the account, you will have to close your account completely. So, the point is, if you're going to add someone as a Joint Account Holder, make sure that it's someone you can TRUST!

Another disadvantage is that most of the time you're only allowed up to 2 joint account holders as opposed to authorized borrower accounts, where in some cases you may have up to 100 authorized borrowers.

Now that you have opened the door to becoming a responsible credit user, after a period of usually six months to a year you can begin to branch off on your own. You can apply for credit cards from places like Macys, Target, J.C. Penny and use them to further build your history. The **revolving credit** from these places is what's called building **Trade Lines**.

4) <u>Increasing Your FICO Score</u>

The abbreviation FICO stands for Fair, Isaac and Company. Its meaning is how lenders determine the manner in which to deal with you as a borrower. Measuring your credit history along with the frequency of credit use is the formula they utilize. The rating often ranges as low as 300 to high as 850. The higher your rating the better the terms will be for you as a borrower. For those with lower ratings, the opposite applies.

EX: Ryan applies and receives a credit card from Macy's for $500. Throughout the first year, he makes nearly a dozen purchases. At the end of each month, he pays off his bill in full. Once the year ended, Ryan's **FICO score** increased significantly. Also because of his timely payments, his spending limit with Macy's increased as well. This make his FICO score increase once again.

5) <u>What Destroys Your Credit</u>

Once your credit is on the road to establishing itself, it becomes essential to understand all the factors that may lead to destroying it. Things like making late payments and **overdrafts** are the most common with credit cards. Going into collections and making **settlements** for debt is even worse. That type of activity will reflect on your credit report for a long time. There have even been instances when lenders have completely washed their hands with a borrower by dismissing an account with bias—meaning that once they settle or close out your account based on debt, they want nothing else to do with you.

LEONARD "SPAR" PERSON JR.

When it comes to property, things like **foreclosures**, **judgments** and **liens** can inflict quite a bit of haunting damage to one's credit.   Even having too many credit cards (more than eight credit cards) or having too many credit checks AKA (Inquiries) in a short period of time can be harmful (**running your credit more than 12 times in a year can reduce your fico score 2 to 3 points each time it's ran**). Another thing to take into account apart from all previously mentioned is not to allow the ratio between your **credit limit** and balance to become too high.

EX: if your credit limit is $500, your balance of debt should never exceed **($250)** half of that amount.

Chapter #2

Looking For The Right Mortgage Program

Now that a history of credit has been created, lenders will have a foundation and boundaries in which to conduct business with you as a borrower. Your next step now towards the world of acquiring property/real estate is to search for the right mortgage program. I mentioned 'search' because this area is an important one. The outcome of the choices made here determines how much of your money will actually go towards purchasing property, how long it will take to pay for it, and at what **interest rate**. There are many types of lending institutions and assisting programs out there to ease the process of becoming a first-time buyer.

LEONARD "SPAR" PERSON JR.

1) <u>What is a Mortgage?</u>

A Mortgage is a loan that constitutes a lien against the **real property**. It usually consists of a two-party agreement between the **lender** and **borrower**. The mortgage pledges a described property as security for the repayment of a loan under certain terms and conditions.

Down below are some of the miscellaneous terms and definitions that **buyers** overlook but are the most important when it comes to receiving a mortgage.

a) <u>Pre-approval</u>

The very first move a borrower has to make to begin this process is to find a mortgage company and seek what's referred to as a **pre-approval**. This is where the mortgage company sets out to determine how much money you as a borrower are eligible to receive from a bank or other lending institution based on income & credit.

b) <u>Grace Period</u>

A **grace period** is a specified time frame after the payment due date in which the payment must be made in order to prevent incurring a late fee. For example, a mortgage may allow a payment due on the first of the month to be paid up until the 15th day of the month without the borrower being in default. (P.S. If you make your payment after the grace period you will be charged a late fee from the bank but, it won't report on your credit report unless your payment is late more than 30 days. By acquiring a late fee this will in some cases prevent you from refinancing your home, give you a higher rate when you do refinance or less of a **LTV** (Loan to Value) when you want to cash out. If you are late more than 30 days then you will get charged a late fee and it will report on your credit report as a late which will drop your score 100s of points. This could possibly prevent you from getting anything ever again. So be an on time payer, or **YOU'RE DONE!**

c) <u>Prepayment Penalty</u>

With the business of real estate thriving, a lot of investors realize that the quicker they can 'flip' a property, the better the profit. This fast buy and sell tactic, although good for the person borrowing money from the bank, isn't so pleasurable for the banks themselves. These sorts of transactions don't allow the banks to profit because the interest they charge to the borrower doesn't get paid due to the short amount of time that the money is being used. As a safety measure, a **clause** has been legally implemented preventing the buyer/borrower of the property to sell or refinance for a specified amount of time. This is done so that the lending institution can profit as well. There are ways around this. If you know that your intentions are just to flip properties, make sure that during negotiation time you specify that you want the **contract** to include that you DON'T want a **prepayment penalty**.

d) <u>Principle, Interest, Taxes, Insurance, PMI and Escrow Accounts</u>

Principal is the amount of money raised by a mortgage or other loan, as distinct from the interest paid on it.

Interest is the money paid for using someone else's money.

LEONARD "SPAR" PERSON JR.

Property Taxes are a government LEVY based on the MARKET VALUE of privately owned property; Sometimes referred to as AD VALOREM TAX or REAL ESTATE TAX.

Insurance is coverage from an insurance company that protects you as a buyer from hazardous damages that may occur when owning a property. Such damages include (but are not limited to) fires, floods, hurricanes, tornados, vandalism to your properties, robberies, jewelry, furniture and certain clothes such as fur coats.

An **Escrow Account for mortgages** is an account for your property taxes and insurance fees attached on top of your mortgage payment and to be paid as one full mortgage payment. This insures the bank that you are definitely keeping your promise of paying your insurance and property taxes.

Private Mortgage Insurance (PMI):

This is an insurance to protect the bank from losing their money that they've financed you, just in case a home owner falls into default with the mortgage. This insurance is paid by the borrower every month in your mortgage payment. **PMI** makes your monthly payment very high but you can have it removed within a year and a half with some banks.

2) Loan Programs

Here are some of the loans that you can qualify for depending on the qualifications of the bank.

P.S. some of these mortgage programs no longer exist since the **SUBPRIME BANKS'** balloon burst in the home finance market. A lot of banks went out of business. Call around to different banks to inquire about these different loan programs and see what the new guidelines and qualifications are.

a) <u>100% Financing Loans</u>

The result of these findings can prove extremely rewarding to certain borrowers after review. Zero money down which is known as 100% financing is offered in some instances when one's income is sufficient joined by an average credit score from the credit bureaus of 700 or better. (This varies from bank to bank).

A popular way in which loans are offered today is through the **80/20** method. This is where the bank loans out two separate loans. Example: If a borrower seeks **100% financing**, instead of the bank just outright lending the money in one lump sum they will provide a loan for 80% for the desired amount. They will then lend out a second loan to cover the remaining

20%. This is usually offered to first-time buyers.

b) <u>Stated Loans</u>

Some borrowers utilize what's called a **Stated Loan**. This type of loan doesn't require the showing of documents like: pay stubs, bank balance, tax returns or W2s etc. To be an eligible applicant of this, your FICO score has to be sufficient. Some lenders however may require certain documents to be completed, such as a **V.O.D.** (**Verification of Deposit**) or 2 months bank statements to show reserves that you at least have 2 to 3 months worth of monthly mortgage payments for emergency; just in case you were to ever default on payments. A **V.O.E.** (**Verification of Employment**) is a form that the bank sends to your employer for them to fill out to verify that your employment is still active **(PS. When verifying your employment the bank is not** allowed to ask the employer how much you make by law. The only thing they can ask is how long you've been employed there and what's your title in the work place). A **V.O.R.** (**Verification of Rent**) is a form that's sent from the bank to your landlord or management company (if you live in an apartment building, co-op or condo) to verify that you live there and how many months or years you've resided there. When verifying your info the bank is allowed to ask how much rent you pay monthly, if you are a good **tenant,** and if you have ever been late in making monthly payments. These 3 documents that I have mentioned (V.O.D., V.O.E., and V.O.R.) prove sufficient holdings in banks, accuracy in employment and place of residence.

The disadvantage of this loan program is that the interest rates are much higher than the other types of loans.

c) <u>Power Options</u>

This leaves the borrower the choice to pay the principal of the loan or the interest. This type of loan is designed for the **investor** who is seeking to buy and re-sell property.

The advantage of the **Option Arm Loan** (**Power Option**) is that your monthly mortgage payment will be beyond low. This gives you room to pay the mortgage and collect a large cash flow every month.

EX: My friend Vernal has a 3 Family house in Brooklyn, New York. Each apartment has 3 bedrooms plus a kitchen and bathroom. The going market rental rate for a 3 bedroom apartment in Brooklyn is $1,500 a month. The total rent roll he collects every month is $4,500. His monthly mortgage is $3,500 and out of that the principle he pays towards the house is $500 dollars the rest of that ($3,000) is interest paid to the bank. Now, with this Option Arm program he has the choice to pay the interest or the principle every month. Of course he chooses to pay the principle to pocket more of the rent role which is $4,500. So he walks away with a profit every month of $4,000.

The disadvantage of this program is that you can only pay that principle or interest for a certain amount of time. If you don't sell your house or refinance for a **fixed rate** within that amount of time, you could owe all of that money you've been deciding not to pay.

EX: My friend Jamel chose to pay the principal ($500) instead of the Interest ($3,000) payment every month, but the terms of that loan was fixed for only 2 years. He lost track and went over the **term time** and forgot to refinance the house for a 30 year fixed rate. Now he owes all of that interest ($72,000) to the bank on top of the principle pay off.

LEONARD "SPAR" PERSON JR.

P.S. Pay Attention to the term time or YOU'RE DONE!

d) <u>Interest Only Loans</u>

This definition is pretty much self explanatory. It's where the borrower pays on the interest of the loan not the principal. This is ideal for the investor or average individual who doesn't plan on keeping the property for a long period of time. If your credit score is at least 700 and you have three active trade lines that you've had for over a year, you can qualify for 100% financing. This may require a V.O.D., V.O.E., and V.O.R. (pgs 55, 56). The advantage of this loan is that you have several payment options and lower monthly payments since you're only paying interest. You're able to borrow more. You can have this loan fixed for up to ten years. This is great if you're not planning to live in it more than ten years. If you and the wife/hubby are planning to have kids and raise them along with the cat, dog, etc, then this is not for you. The end result could be foreclosure and your home could end up for sale at the auction and I might just be the one buying it back again.

e) FHA Loans

The **Department of Housing and Urban Development** (**HUD**) is the agency responsible for the policies and programs that address America's housing needs. HUD plays a major role in home ownership by underwriting loans for low/moderate income families. The **Federal Housing Administration** (**FHA**) assists those who otherwise would be able to meet the requirement for **down payment** or conventional loans by providing mortgage insurance to private lenders. Everyone who has a satisfactory credit record, enough cash to close the loan, and sufficient steady income to make monthly mortgage payments can be approved for an FHA insured mortgage. To get an FHA insured loan you need to apply with a HUD approved lender. FHA loans are available in urban areas for single family homes, two, three, and even four unit properties. This is true for condominiums as well. The interest rates are generally market rates while down payment requirements are lower than conventional loans. Down payments can be as low as three percent and closing costs can be wrapped into the mortgage. With an FHA insured mortgage, you can make extra payments towards the principal when you make your regular monthly payments. By making extra payments you can repay the loan faster and save on interest. You can also pay off the entire balance of the FHA insured at any time.

LEONARD "SPAR" PERSON JR.

f) <u>Fixed Rate Mortgage</u>

These rates come in 15, 30, 40, and in some situations 50 year terms. The advantage of this loan is that your monthly payments are fixed for the lifetime of the loan. So when interest rates fluctuate your rates will remain the same as when you first purchased the property. If the rates go down, you have the advantage of refinancing your loan to obtain a better rate. If this happens, make sure you get a better fixed rate and not an adjustable one or you will end up having to refinance again. The disadvantage to all of this is that because it is a fixed rate your rate and mortgage payment will be higher.

My opinion about **fixed rate mortgages** is if you're planning to reside in a home for a significantly long time, for example 30 years or until you leave this world, then a fixed rate mortgage is the right choice for you.

LEONARD "SPAR" PERSON JR.

This way you can obtain a good rate in the beginning and it will never change. As long as you can maintain your monthly payments you will be okay. If you only plan to reside in the home for a short period of time (1-3 years or 3-5 years), you will be better off with a different type of loan program. I'm going to get into that shortly.

g) Adjustable Rate Mortgages

This type of loan is available for 1, 3, 5 or 10 years with the most common ones being 3 to 10 years. The advantages are that you will receive lower monthly rates and if overall rates improve it will bring your rate down as well. You may qualify for a higher loan amount because of the **adjustable rate**. There are also no **balloon payments** involved. Keep in mind there are disadvantages. The rates can change over time, if overall rates go up your rate will be affected. For example just say you get an adjustable rate on a house for three or five years. Your interest rate is 5%. After the 5 years is up, you are then subjected to the **market rate**. At that point you have the option of selling the home or refinancing and getting a fixed rate, So think carefully before you get this type of loan. My opinion is, if you plan on staying for a long time a fixed rate is best for you. Anything shorter than that, go with the adjustable. Investors who are constantly buying and selling are prone to this type of loan.

h) Balloon Mortgages

This means low payments are going to be lower payments for a pre-determined period of time. It offers an option to renew the loan at the end of the specified term. It's normally 5 to 7 years. The disadvantage here is that you risk the interest rate being higher at the end of the agreement term. You can find yourself easily in foreclosure if you can't make the loan payments, refinance, or for not exercising the conversion **clause**. Balloon payments allow you to sell or refinance the house opposed to a fixed rate loan with a 30 year term. The catch is that once the term ends you HAVE to either refinance or sell because if the interest rate goes up drastically then the mortgage payment amounts may become a problem. Bottom line; if you're an investor looking to buy and sell then this is for you;–otherwise avoid this type of loan situation.

i) First Time Homebuyers

This has a very low rate and is very easy to get approved for. You may be subject though to income and property value limitations. You may be required to sign a pre-payment penalty agreement which prevents you from selling or refinancing the property for a specified amount of time. This ensures the lender that they will make their money off of the interest. You will have to get a summary course on the different types of loans which shouldn't be a problem because you should do your research before you buy anything. Now-a-days, your Fico has to be at least a 700 to obtain 100% financing for approval for the 80/20 loan program. That leaves a lot of available cash on hand to put into the hole. If you understand all of this you will be okay because for the first time homebuyer it is great.

j) No Point-No Fee Program

This arrangement has no out of pocket cost at closing. Costs are paid from the **lender rebate /discount points**, and less money is required to close. You can refinance without increasing your loan amount. All of this is very good. Again, the disadvantage is the high interest rate, higher payment, and some lenders have what is called a **short payoff penalty**. This is usually charged to the loan **broker** but may be passed on to you. Some require prepayment penalty for the first 1-5 years. The bottom line to all of these different types of loans and programs is that they offer an array of different options to sometimes benefit the buyer if they know what they're actually looking for. All in all, in order to receive, you have to give a little.

k) Imperfect Credit Program

Through this avenue, you have the opportunity to re-establish your credit status by paying your mortgage on time. The new history will help you a great deal because it reflects on your credit report. You can also use this if you go for debt consolidation. When a bank is considering your eligibility for this program, your Debt to Income Ratio on your credit report must be under a certain percentage (usually 50% - 55%). The disadvantages again are the high interest rates and terms may not be as favorable. You have to realize that you have imperfect credit from the start. The overall good thing about this is that although you have bad credit, you can still buy a home. Just say if you come across a home for $200,000 but it's really worth $400,000. You can use this program, but just know that the interest rates will be higher than normal. Even though you will have a prepayment penalty on your loan, once you sell the house and pay off the loan and prepayment penalty, you'll still walk away with a stack of money. The point is, when you have an opportunity to buy an **investment property**, programs like Imperfect Credit can still help you succeed.

LEONARD "SPAR" PERSON JR.

I) <u>Home Equity Line Of Credit</u>

This loan is for people that already own a property. The basis of this loan is that you only borrow what you need. You pay interest only on what you borrow. The interest may be **tax deductible** and you may be free from closing costs. This can also serve as an excellent source of emergency income if set up in advance. It can also help you consolidate your debt and lower your personal monthly payments (ex: credit cards, car notes, etc.). The terms of the loan are more favorable than if you take out a regular loan. Example: if you have $100,000 **equity** in your home and you borrow say $50,000. You would only have to pay interest on the $50,000. And say out of the $50,000 you only end up using $20,000, you will then be required to pay interest only on the $20,000. You don't have to pay any closing costs to borrow the money. The disadvantage is that the interest rate can change, making your payments higher. This is reflected by the fluctuating market rate. Getting an approval for a Refinance is harder for first time homebuyers as well.

m) <u>Refinancing</u>

This loan is for the property owner who is repaying at a rate which most likely was unfavorable to them because they didn't meet all of the necessary requirements to receive a more suitable loan. Now that time has passed, they have accumulated home equity, better credit, etc, so they can go back to the bargaining table and take out a new loan with better terms and rates to offset the earlier loan. Some people go this route to cash out on the savings left over. Others just want to lower their interest rates. Here you also have to pay closing costs all over again.

LEONARD "SPAR" PERSON JR.

This will take money from your equity.

*Note: If you are seeking a loan for a property, contact us at www.hoodestate.com or dial 1.800.699.7020.

Chapter #3
Purchasing The Right Property

Having great style is a fantastic characteristic to possess when it comes to clothing and cars. When it balls down to property, you have to be cautious on what just looks good. Choosing the right property is a skilled task--similar to a diamond collector on the hunt for the right stones. In his or her quest, they know exactly what and what not to look for in making their purchase. Things like cut, clarity and carat will determine the current and future holding value in his stones. A person investing in property looks for certain key things when determining what type of real estate to acquire. One of the main points is the size of the property. Go to www.propertyshark.com. This is a great website to obtain foreclosed property and property going into foreclosure. It gives the names and contact number of the **seller** of the property. Through them you can get authorization from the seller to contact the bank or lender who has the property in foreclosure so that you can negotiate a steal on the buyout. This can prove to be profitable because the lender now has a chance to cash out on the defaulted property instead of risking going to an auction and receiving less. The lender may not accept your first offer but will counter offer until you've both reached a mutual agreement.

1) <u>MULTI-UNITS</u>

This type of property refers to anything more than a single residence but less that a five family. Ex: A two or three-family home can be considered a **multi-unit** as well as a building containing four individual apartments. Anything beyond that is a **commercial unit**. The profitability of this is reasonable and can generate enough cash through renting to pay for itself. When purchasing a multi-unit there are key points to look for.

1) How many bedrooms are in each apartment? (Having a lot of bedrooms equals more rent-roll!)

2) The plumbing and electric must be in working condition

3) How old is the boiler? (If boiler is over 10 years old it might need to be replaced or upgraded.)

4) How old is the roof and does it need to be replaced? (If the roof has present leaks or is more than 25 years old, then it should be replaced).

5) What are the highest value sales in the area that is comparable to your house? (Just in case you run into a financial situation and you might need to sell quick, make sure you have

enough room in the house (**equity**) to sell and make a profit as well). If these outlooks work out in your favor then this could be a good deal for you depending on the price of the home.

ADVANTAGES OF OWNING A MULTI-UNIT

One ADVANTAGE of owning a Multi-unit is that you can collect a good rental cash flow depending on how many apartments you have within the house and how many bedrooms each apartment has in it. The location also matters when it comes to getting top dollar rent roll for your rental. Another advantage is:

If you're moving into a property that's a multi-unit, the rent roll from the additional apartment(s) can either cover the whole mortgage or at least help with a good portion of your mortgage payments. The point is, you will definitely be paying less out of your pocket.

DISADVANTAGES OF OWNING A MULTI-UNIT

> (1) Expenses are higher than a one family home. (Water, Heat, Electricity, etc)
>
> (2) You're responsible for all tenants and maintenance of the building.
>
> (3) When you're ready to sell the property, having it occupied makes it difficult to sell fast.

2) <u>Commercial Units and Mix-Use Properties</u>

This is where the property contains space to hold more than five separate families. Projects, high rises or any building possessing more than five apartments/offices/stores are prime examples of **commercial** property. A **mix-use property** will have a 2 or 3 family that has a store front. The profitability of this can be substantially rewarding. Being that it holds more **occupancies** and commercial business space, it can generate enough income to pay for itself and hefty profit.

ADVANTAGES OF A COMMERCIAL UNIT & MIX-USE PROPERTY

(1) The rent roll/cash flow is more rewarding than a multi-family or single residence property

(2) It has space to put a commercial business which creates an opportunity for entrepreneurship and an additional income along with your monthly rent roll.

DISADVANTAGES OF COMMERCIAL   UNIT & MIX-USE

(1) Huge monthly utility and housing expenses.

(2) Some commercial businesses operated out of the premises may need a license to operate, such as: restaurants, sports bars, clubs, etc. This can become a huge expense in the beginning but will be very profitable in the long run.

(3) Refinancing a commercial property or mix-use property can be difficult.

(4) Selling a commercial property can be difficult as well because buyers are obligated to put a down payment of at least 20-25% of the purchase price and not everyone has that amount of cash available to them. Therefore it may take a longer time to sell.

3) <u>Foreclosures</u>

Now that you are familiar with some of the basic types of property, we're going to move on to how you can actually buy them. Property is sold and bought in many ways; directly from the owner, through or from a bank, from Real Estate Brokers & Investment companies, etc. The most popular way in which some properties are sought after today is by foreclosure. **Foreclosure** is when the bank seeks to take possession of the property from the owner after lack of several payments on the loan. This type of action brought against the owner places a person seeking to buy property a hefty advantage. They can either wait until the bank has taken possession of the property to attempt to buy it or can seek to bail out the owner on a buyout by picking up the payments minus the equity.

LEONARD "SPAR" PERSON JR.

EX.: My boy Damon owns a house in Bedford-Stuyvesant (Brooklyn, NY) and he is backed up in his mortgage payments by 6 months. He owes a mortgage of $300,000 and his 6 months of backed up payments is $10,000. His house is worth $550,000. I suggested that he give me the bank's number so that I could contact the bank and buy into his mortgage. How this works is that, the bank will have to check my credit and financial records to see if I am pre-approved to qualify for a mortgage. Then if I am eligible, I'll pay off the $10,000 default payments he owes to the bank and then take over the mortgage and the ownership of the property. Four months later, I sold the property and made a profit of about $240,000 and only invested $10,000 (his 6 months of default payments) to make that profit. This makes sense to do only if the property has a huge amount of equity in it and the monthly mortgage payments are reasonable enough for you to handle. (Now, where else can you invest $10,000 and make $240,000 in 4 months???)

4) <u>**Buying 3 Properties At Once**</u>

Sounds like a dream come true? Well it's a reality and people do it all the time. How? For first time home buyers there are several benefits offered by banks and other lending institutions. The simple fact that you qualify for first time home buyer loan programs itself is enough to cover this area. What the borrower would do in this case is simply use your excellent credit, go to three different banks and acquire loans to purchase the properties. The key here is that it has to be done right after one another, before the Credit Bureaus (Equifax, Experian & TransUnion) report your first loan and the banks realize that you have actually taken out several loans. If the banks would've noticed that you have another home loan already, you wouldn't qualify for a first time home buyer loan program. It's legal so what are you waiting for – go for it!!

5) <u>**Short Sale Properties**</u>

This technique of purchasing a property before it goes into foreclosure is one of the greatest profitable purchases you can make in Real Estate. A Short Sale occurs when a property is in the beginning stages of foreclosure. This is beneficial to both the bank and the potential buyer (YOU) because you get to buy the property for cheaper than what the last owner purchased it for and the bank doesn't stand to lose as much money as they would if the property gets auctioned off. Here's how it works:

(a) You get the owner to sign a **Letter of**

Authorization which basically says that the owner gives the bank permission to discuss and release information about their loan to you.

(b) You contact the bank and ask for the **Loss Mitigation Department** to find the person assigned to this specific loan account. You let the assigned specialist know what property you are calling on behalf of, tell them that you are interested in doing a **Short Sale** and that you have a Letter of Authorization from the owner that you are prepared to fax to them.

(c) Once you've faxed them the Letter of Authorization the seller's(owner) lawyer has to submit a **legal binding contract** between the buyer (YOU) and the seller

LEONARD "SPAR" PERSON JR.

(Owner) , and a **Good Faith Estimate HUD 1** to the bank. The contract will contain your offer price for the property. The Good Faith Estimate HUD1 basically breaks down all of the numbers and expenses and gives the bank an idea of how much money they will be able to clear. Your offer price will definitely be lower than the amount that the owner owes. (Before you submit your papers with your offer price make sure you find out exactly how much the seller owes the bank {ex. $550,000})

(d) Once these papers are submitted you have to wait and see if the bank approves your offer. The bank will counter offer if it doesn't accept your offer and you will negotiate with the bank until you come to a mutual agreement. .

(e) Once the offer is accepted you begin your Loan process.

6) <u>Tax Certificates</u>

This a document that certifies money/taxes owed by a property owner. There are two ways to acquire these certificates. It varies from state to state. You can go to auctions. Also you can go to land listings and purchase certificates that haven't been bought at the auctions. Once you have the **tax certificate**, this is how it works; ex: Say you bought a certificate for $1,000 against a property. Now the property owner owes you that $1,000 plus interest which falls in the form of a **tax lien** against the property. Depending on the laws governing from state to state, the **redemption**

period can vary anywhere from 3 months to 2 years. Bottom line, if the debt isn't paid by the required time, the property owner will lose his property to the certificate holder for the said amount. Meaning, a person can lose a $300,000 home for a mere $1,000.

7)   <u>People You Know That Own Property</u>

Another great way to acquire property is by purchasing it from someone you know. Whether it is a family member, friend, colleague or drinking buddy, buying property from someone that you personally know will most certainly provide some sort of bargain.

"Chapter #4"

Submitting An Offer

Negotiating a price for a specific property takes savvy and know how. The owner of the property will ask for a certain amount based on current property value rate, time & money invested, among other factors. You as the buyer will naturally go for the best price possible by counter offering. That's just how business goes.

1) Submitting an Offer Sheet

Once you have decided on an offer price you must fill out and submit an **offer sheet** to the real estate broker for that property. The broker will present the offer to the seller at which time it is the seller's decision to accept the offer or not. The broker will then contact you and let you know the seller's decision. If the seller accepts your offer, you will start the loan process.

2) Denied Offer

Again, after the owner of the property has heard your offer, he/she may either accept or deny it. If he/she denies it, you will have to **counter offer** through strong negotiation. If persuasive enough, you may talk him/her into selling for a better price.

3) Getting An Inspection

Just like when buying anything, you always checkout the merchandise before finalizing the purchase. Just like you wouldn't buy a car without making sure the engine is running properly; you have to bring in a professional to inspect certain aspects of the property.

The main points to focus on are; the roof, the presence of lead, and the boiler. If there is a problem with any of these three things, then they need to be pointed out and dealt with beforehand.

LEONARD "SPAR" PERSON JR.

"Chapter #5"

Collecting Cash Flow From Property

Take a moment out to congratulate yourself on officially becoming a property owner, but don't take too long because there is money to be made!

Depending on the quantity and type of property you've acquired, your rate of income is about to change. You as an owner want to make sure that the level of income is as fruitful as possible.

1) Working People Rentals

If you want to rent out space but at the same time keep things simple and traditional, you can rent out your property to ordinary working people for a set monthly price. If the property is decent enough the money charged will hopefully cover the mortgage, insurance and utility costs and maybe at the end of the day will yield you some sort of profit.

a) The advantage of renting to people that work is as long as they're working you can receive your money on time. If they have a good job where they receive raises and bonuses you may just be able to go up on the rent every year. Working tenants are a lot more responsible and reliable than government assistance program services.

For EX: One of my tenants in my building was on a **Section 8** program; the others were working class people. I always got the rent from the working family with no problem, but the Section 8 Department staff doesn't speak to landlords if the tenant's rent isn't up to date with you in some cases. That was a major problem because the Section 8 tenant and I had problems and we weren't on good terms, so to make a long story short the Section 8 Department put a stop on my check, and even when the tenant and I resolved our issues it still took months for them to reimburse me the rent. I had to pay out of my pocket for those additional months.

b) The disadvantage is if the working class person loses their jobs, unfortunately you take a lost as well. And the scary part about that is you never know when your job is going to fire you, so nothing is guaranteed or lasts forever.

2) <u>Government Program Rentals</u>

Some property owners come to find out that by renting property to the normal working class leaves them vulnerable to dealing directly with tenants.

Collecting rent can become a real hassle if a tenant decides not to pay for whatever reason and you as the owner can not evict them without going through the legal process.

An alternative to avoid this is to rent out space to tenants, but not directly. Instead, you contract your property out to the Federal Government for a set fee. They in turn will fill the property with tenants who are eligible for federal assistance. This is called **subsidized housing**.

For EX: I rented out one of my apartments to a federal program called Section 8. The good thing about this program is that they paid me first month's rent, security and they were always on time with payment. I never had to go to the tenant in person and ask for my rent. I also didn't have to worry about the tenant having a job or losing their job because everything was funded by the government.

The disadvantage of this program is when you start the process of registering your building for approval, it can take from 4 to 6 months to get approved. First you have to view and interview every tenant. Then you have to order a Section 8 inspection which takes almost 2 weeks for the inspectors to come out to your property; And god forbid if you miss them the first time you have to reorder the inspection and that's another 2 week wait. After that you can move the tenant in but even then you don't receive the check because you will have to wait until your application is fully processed and that could take up to 3 months. Basically you have to have 4 months of mortgage payments saved up to follow this program through. The only good thing is after your application is processed they will reimburse you for all the months they didn't pay.

3) <u>Single Room Occupancy Rentals</u>

This option if done safe and correctly, can be very profitable. You can take a piece of sufficient property and restructure it to accommodate several different tenants. They will each have the privacy of their own room and may share the bathroom and kitchen areas.

P.S. Make sure the Property is **S.R.O** (**Single Room Occupancy**) certified.   This allows you to rent out rooms legal without breaking the law because the house was built and registered for that purpose to rent only rooms. If the house's **C of O** (**Certificate of Occupancy**) is a 1, 2, 3, 4, 5 family, commercial or mix use then you are not allowed to rent rooms by law.

4) <u>Home Daycare Programs</u>

Here for the new millennium caring for senior citizens and children has become one of the fastest rising businesses. With parents and family members having to work, they don't have the time or resources to stay at home and care for their loved ones, so this service has come to the rescue. If you, the person you're renting to and your property qualify, you can create an entity that caters to the children/elderly. You can do this privately or through contractual work for the State of Federal Government. Keep in mind that when it comes to caring for people, regulations are very strict. You can and will be fined for the simplest of things. If not corrected and enforced you will be shut down and barred from daycare completely. So don't just look at this as money in the bank if your professionalism isn't up to par. In order to successfully reap the vast wealth in this area you will have to stay on top of things.

a) The advantage of this program is that, when qualified, the government pays you up to $150 to $200 a week per kid. Depending on what type of program you choose to do, you could have from 6 to 12 kids in your home daycare. The government also gives you educational **money vouchers** for computers, learning appliances, toys, **food vouchers** for breakfast, lunch, snack and dinner. Now let us do the math assuming you are getting top dollar ($200) from all 12 kids. You will be making a gross profit of $2400 a week and $9600 a month, and that's only for one apartment in a 3 family building. There are still 2 more apartments that you can rent out and receive more cash flow.

LEONARD "SPAR" PERSON JR.

5) Senior Citizen Rentals

In many cases, elderly people refuse to be dropped off in some old folks home, (as they call it). They'd rather spend their time alone in the comfort of their own apartment specially designed for them. Most of these types of establishments have around the clock monitoring staff and the apartments are equipped to accommodate their needs and limited ability. Because of the level of personalization, living arrangements of this sort can provide a property owner with considerable income.

P.S. There are other Government programs you can register your building under to collect a cash flow like DAS (HIV Tenants), Jiggits (rental assistance) and domestic violence shelters for woman. To get more information about these programs go to a official

LEONARD "SPAR" PERSON JR.

government website EX: (www.nyc.gov)

"Chapter #6"

Selling Your Property

Owning a piece of property doesn't necessarily mean that you will always keep it. Not that you can't, but for many different reasons you may just not want to. In those instances, you will move to sell. Depending on the type of property you own, the condition that it's in and the financial status that it's under you may have to go a certain route in order to successfully find a buyer.

1) Renovation Sale

If the property that you have isn't in the best living conditions, fixing the place up will surely make your task of selling much easier. This type of action is very common and has proven to be successful. Someone looking to buy property wants nothing more than to acquire something already up to standards. The more luxury your renovations are the more money you can ask for to rent the location. The key rooms to renovate in a house or apartment is the kitchen and bathroom. These rooms are the eye catchers, especially when you have company or if you want to sell your property and receive top value.

The Disadvantage of renovating a property is dealing with contractors that aren't consistent, loyal, professional or licensed. You might try to save money by dealing with a family member or friend whom you know that does contracting work and is willing to give you a better deal of course. The thing is, since you have some type of relationship with them, it's not based on business anymore and sometimes your kindness get taking for weakness. Before you know it, you've spent more than what you budgeted and the work still isn't

LEONARD "SPAR" PERSON JR.

finish.

My advice to you is to go with the professional contractors that have a good track record and can get the job done. You might end up paying $100's more in the beginning but will save $1000's at the end with the work done in a timely fashion.

For EX: I remember when I bought my one family home in New Jersey. I tried to save money by getting my dad and father-in-law to do the work. It took damn near 9 to 11 months for them to renovate my house and it still isn't finished til' this day. I am grateful to have had them in my corner anyway but damn, I spent over 125k and the contractors were only going to charge me 75k to 80k to renovate the whole property within 4 to 5 months in the beginning. But one thing I could say about my dad and father-in-law is that they stood by me until the end and made sure the work was done with quality and not rushed.

P.S. Dad (When are you going to finish my shit Lenny?) LOL! Bats I still owe you $5,000 but can you put my closet poles up, I'm tired of putting my clothes in garbage bags...LOL!

2) <u>Vacant Sale</u>

At the time of sale, your property may or may not be occupied with tenants. This factor has a lot of bearing on the sale itself. Vacant property is always easier to sell, although selling occupied property is not impossible. It really depends on the intentions of the buyer.

The advantage of buying vacant property is that you as a buyer do not have to inherit bad tenants. You don't have to rebuild a relationship with them or be looked at as the new enemy on the block. For example: you might bring to their attention a new set of rules like increasing their rent and because they're so use to paying what they've been paying for so many years it will probably become a problem collecting your rent in the beginning

3) <u>Occupied Sale</u>

When the property is occupied with tenants this can work for you or against you, as far as price negotiations are concerned. Some buyers are nit picky about inheriting tenants, especially ones they don't know anything about. This can cause a mountain of future problems. For example: any promises made by the previous owner will for sure also be inherited as well. On the other hand, the buyer may welcome the fact that there are tenants already in place. Now the issue of finding tenants is out the window. With this rent load, the purchased property can immediately begin paying for itself.

4) "As Is" Sale

Plainly put, it is what it is. What you see is what you get. The owner puts out a price, the buyer checks out the place and makes his or her decision. Take it or leave it.

5) Foreclosure Sale

What's being done here is not actually a foreclosure sale. The potential buyer in this instance is seeking to acquire the property before the foreclosure takes place. Knowing that the owner is in a financial jam, the buyer will bail out the owner by paying off the debt and taking possession of the property.

How to get out of foreclosure: There are 2 ways you can get out of a foreclosure situation.

a) Deed Transfer

How this works is when you fall in default with the mortgage payment you should look for someone you trust with good credit and a good financial income record to add them onto your **deed**. The **deed transfer** can be done with a real estate attorney. It usually cost around $450 to $500 for this transaction and can be active in 2 weeks, depending on what attorney you're dealing with. By connecting this person to your deed you're giving them 50% ownership of your property and this gives them the legal right to refinance the property to pay off the existing default mortgage and get you out of foreclosure. (The good thing is that the person you add on can't do anything without your signature, but the bad thing is that it goes both ways, you can't do anything without their signature as well). This person can't be a family member, but can be a friend. They also can't have the same last name as you because the bank considers that a conflict of interest and a bail out. (No family members)

b) <u>Giving the Property Back to the Bank</u>

This is pretty much self explanatory. If you know that you are about to default on your mortgage due to monetary problems, (EX: losing your job, losing your tenants, family issues, etc.) you should alert the bank in advance that you can no longer afford to maintain the mortgage note. The bank will make arrangements to either repossess the property or work out some type of payment arrangement with you (This is optional, not all banks will agree to payment arrangements).

If the bank does agree to work out a payment arrangement, that will be good on your behalf. It will prevent your credit from being destroyed. You will have a second chance.

P.S. If you do have a family member willing to do a deed transfer, just make sure you don't have the same last name. Also the smart thing to do is after the transaction is completed and your foreclosure is paid off and settled you should remove that person from the deed to take back 100% ownership of your property. To remove them you have to follow the same procedure that you used to add them onto the deed through an attorney's supervision. You can't just sign them off yourself; they have to sign off willingly.

LEONARD "SPAR" PERSON JR.

"Chapter #7"

Flipping Properties

In today's real estate market, it seems like the name of the game is the "**quick flip**". Buyers are on the hunt for anything that they can get their paws on so that they can do whatever's necessary to turn around, sell and make that quick profit. To come out on top, you have to know how to move. This means looking in a prime and safe location to buy a flip property and when to strike...

1) Buying Under Market Value

Many times while out on the prowl you will stumble upon property that you will be able to buy below and sometimes even well below its current market value. Maybe the property needs considerable work done and

LEONARD "SPAR" PERSON JR.

the owner doesn't have the cash but in turn needs cash. There are many case scenarios where the owner may be willing to get rid of the property for a price that is a steal on your end.

2) Buyers Lined Up To Buy From You

Some buyers do things with considerable foresight-premeditation. When they buy, they already have someone lined up or in mind to re-sell to. Having a buyer lined up, is perhaps the true meaning of a quick flip. You acquire the property for a negotiated price and sell it to make a profit.

3) Assigned Contract

The art of buying and selling property for the quick flip isn't always as easy as it appears. When buying the property, you have to let the previous owner know what your intentions are. Better yet, you should have your attorney state that in the contract so that there won't be any misunderstandings down the road. Here with an **assigned contract**, you will be obtaining the property more or less as a middle man only to buy it and then sell it to the end buyer. That's why it is essential that the original seller is aware of what's going on.

4) <u>Auction Properties</u>

State, Federal Government and other agencies at certain times of the year auction off numerous amounts of prime real estate. These events are great opportunities to grab property at incredible prices. If you're an average person looking for a home, then that could be the ideal place for you. For buyers that are seeking to buy multiple properties for the purpose of financial gain, you have to possess certain credentials in order to do so.

LEONARD "SPAR" PERSON JR.

"Chapter #8"

Choosing The Right Lawyer

When dealing with a market such as real estate, choosing the right lawyer makes all the difference in the world. A lot of contracts filled with technical jargon are involved and a lawyer with skill and common sense is necessary. The relationship you two share will have a strong bearing on your level of success.

1) Choose A Lawyer That Deals Directly With Real Estate

You have many types of attorneys out there; Criminal, Civil, Entertainment, etc. You even have some that deal with more than one field. Make sure the one you choose specializes in real estate. Do not accept the 'dibbing and dabbing' lawyer who tries to juggle different hats.

2) <u>Research A Lawyer's Track Record</u>

In order to be certain that a lawyer is the right one for you, you must check him out. You have to check his/her track record for competence, professionalism, etc. Ask the lawyer for references; old and current clients, so you can do your search with the Bar Association. Usually they will have the answers you are looking for.

3) <u>Consistency</u>

Just like a ship in motion full stream ahead, so should be the consistency of your lawyer's actions. He should be prompt with his duties and complete what he says he can get done. In real estate you don't need any unforeseeable red tape and if your lawyer is on top of his/her job then you rarely will.

4) Lawyers Can Blow Deals

Prompt response and attention to a matter or deal is a requisite of a good attorney. Deals worth hundreds of thousands and sometimes millions have went down the drain or slipped out of an investor's hands due to untimely and lack of proper attention. This most often becomes the case when a lawyer has a large roster of clients and/or too much work on his/her plate. Also, not to seem bias or racist, but when dealing with lawyers of certain backgrounds, a vast amount of time off from work due to religious worship can conflict with business that needs a sharp response. So you have to choose your lawyer wisely.

LEONARD "SPAR" PERSON JR.

"Chapter #9"

"Finding The Right Appraiser"

The whole purpose of getting involved in the world of real estate is to make the most money off of a property. To accomplish that, you need have some type of understanding about negotiating and be familiar with the legalities of the real estate market. You have to also evaluate the property that you seek to acquire. If the property is no good or isn't worth investing time and money into as far as renovations, then you stand to lose. The person that can ensure that you come out on top with property worthwhile is called an **Appraiser**. This individual or sometimes, team of individuals, come in and analyze the actual worth of the property in question. An **appraisal**, which is the outcome of their findings, will let you know whether the deal is really a deal or not.

LEONARD "SPAR" PERSON JR.

1) <u>Looking For The Best Market Value</u>

Competence is a must when choosing an appraiser. Anything short of that and you will pay dearly. There are so many things to consider when determining if a piece of property holds or has the potential to mature to its best market value. He/she has to be able to see beyond the surface of the game. Key factors when looking for property are square footage, number of units, compared to the price. When the appraiser does comparisons in that particular area, this will determine the best deal in relation to current market value.

2) <u>Consistent Work In A Timely Fashion</u>

You need an appraiser that's going to come out and do his/her job and not waste your time. Their duty is to show up on time and appraise the said property in an efficient manner. Be thorough when seeking an appraiser because the evaluations that he/she will make on your property will determine whether or not actual profitability exists.

3) Paying Half Up Front/Rest At Closing

For satisfying results, they should be paid on the spot upon completion of the task or half up front and the balance once they're finish. This process has always proven to stimulate motivation when it comes down to work for hire.

4) Building A Strong Relationship

More than just an understanding will be required when dealing with an appraiser. A bond is more so needed. His/her duties are extremely critical to you.

An appraiser must know what it is that you're trying to accomplish from any said piece of property and evaluate according to your standards. If that connection is made in a respectable and efficient manner then you as an investor will always remain ahead of the game.

5) <u>Specializing In The Area Being Appraised</u>

Bottom line; an appraiser needs to be familiar with the area being appraised. He/she should also have experience with the specific types of property in question. Despite the types of software available today, it will be of little use if no personal knowledge is there to support. Take heed to this because if not you will be wasting a lot of your valuable time and money.

6) <u>Gathering The Right Data</u>

When dealing with appraisers, make certain that they are compiling accurate and relevant information when evaluating the property. This is one of the most common errors being made today. Lack of proper research will offset the true value of the sought property leading to possibly a very bad investment.

TIP: HOW APPRAISERS DETERMINE THE VALUE OF A PROPERTY

The appraiser has to look for 3 comparable houses that have been sold in the past 3 to 6 months, in the area he/she is appraising. They usually compare homes that are within a mile of the property and that are the same amount of families and are around the same square feet. Once the appraise finds the comparable homes (known as Comps), he/she bases the value of the property on how much all 3 homes were sold for in that area within the past 6 months or year.

LEONARD "SPAR" PERSON JR.

For Example:

Sandy bought her home for $300K in 2004. It is a 2 family home with 2,800 square feet. She decides that she wants to refinance and pull some cash out. Her home is appraised for $600K because the appraiser was able to find 3 comps within a mile that were 2 family homes with similar square footage that had recently sold for $600k.

LEONARD "SPAR" PERSON JR.

"Chapter # 10"
Choosing The Right Title Company

This area of expertise is necessary as a means of protection. It lets the parties involved know that you are knowledgeable and cautious. When going into any deal of purchasing property, those attributes need to be felt front and center. A title search protects you from inheriting any judgments, tax liens or defaults that the seller may have against them or the property.

1) **Getting a Title Search & Title Insurance**

Basically all you have to do is look for a company that performs **title searches** and **title insurance**. This insures you against buying property from someone that claims to be the owner of the property but then down the line you come to find out otherwise. This also protects you from the loan that was taken out from the bank and all the other steps you put forth to acquire the property.

2) <u>Schedule A</u>

This is a file that is created from doing a research/financial background check on the buyer and seller. This will bring up any issues of child support, alimony, liens or judgments that exist; and sometimes down to parking tickets. This area has to be addressed before clearance is given to close on a deal.

3) <u>Low Fees</u>

Like with shopping for anything, you will always seek and compare prices when looking for a **title company**. Warning: Do not allow better pricing to compromise quality and service. Doing this will defeat your whole purpose.

4) <u>Trustworthiness With Escrow Accounts</u>

In the process of the title company ensuring that you, as the buyer, do not inherit any type of judgment, liens, fees, etc, there will come a time where the buyer and seller will disagree on something that was made clear earlier on and has become an issue at the time of closing. For example: the seller may have promised the buyer that at the time of closing there wouldn't be any tenants occupying the property but when the time came to close, the tenants were still there. Or something was agreed upon to have been repaired by the time of **closing** but hasn't been fixed. These discrepancies would call for an **escrow account** to be created in which the seller would deposit a certain amount of cash there to compensate for the matter at hand. The title company would hold onto this money until the specified date the buyer and seller agreed upon that their matter would be addressed. If the matter wasn't addressed, then the title company would have been required to relinquish the money over to the buyer as compensation. Be weary of the title company who has done business with the seller previously and may have an ongoing relationship. If a thorough reference check on the title company isn't done, you may find yourself receiving the short end of the stick.

LEONARD "SPAR" PERSON JR.

"Chapter # 11"
What Are Closing Costs?

This is a cost of many fees that you have to pay when borrowing money from a bank to purchase property. It extends from **mortgage taxes** to **transfer taxes** to **mortgage broker's fees**, etc. To cover these costs, sometimes the buyer will seek a larger loan from the bank to cover it, instead of coming out of their pockets. The seller/owner has to approve of this in order for it to be accepted. This is called a **seller's concession**.

1) HUD 1

This is a giant, legal document that breaks everything down to the exact dollar and cents. It includes every transaction of the closing costs between the buyer and seller. So if you want to know if the seller and any other party involved actually made a profit from the property, you can look there.

2) Transfer Taxes

This fee is paid to the government whenever the deed of a property is transferred from one party to another. (Uncle Sam has his hand in everything).

3) Mortgage Taxes

This is a tax that has to be paid by the buyer to cover taxes charged to the **mortgage broker**.

4) Mortgage Broker's Fees

The mortgage broker makes his/her money by searching for a lender who will loan you the money to purchase the home. For example; In New York they charge on an average, 3% of the loan amount for their services. In other states, the **points** charged by the brokers are either higher or lower.

5) <u>Pay-Off</u>

This is directed to the seller. If he/she had a previous mortgage or an old gas, electric or water bill, he/she will be required to pay it off. This includes any left over property taxes

6) <u>Broker's Commission And Title Fees</u>

Broker's commission is a fee paid by the seller and it is derived from the proceeds from selling the property. **Title fees** are paid by the buyer for all the services that were previously mentioned in the earlier paragraph on the title company.

LEONARD "SPAR" PERSON JR.

HOOD ESTATE GLOSSARY

A

Adjustable-Rate Mortgage (ARM) - A mortgage loan that allows the *interest rate* to be changed at specific periods over the maturity of the loan. Also known as *Power Option* or *ARM* loan.

Appraisal - A professional opinion or estimate of the value of the property. Also, the act or process of estimating value.

    Example: A property owner may have an *appraisal* made of a specific property to:

- determine a reasonable offering price in a sale
- Determine the value at death for estimate tax purposes
- Determine the amount of hazardous insurance to

carry

- Allocate the purchase price to the land and improvements

Appraiser - One qualified to estimate the value of real property.

    Example: One may hire an *appraiser* to render an opinion of a property's market value just before they purchase the property

Approval - A letter from the bank stating that you are approved for a specified loan amount.

"As Is" Sale - A sale of a property without guarantees as to condition. Premises are accepted by a buyer or tenant as they are, including physical defects.

Assigned Contract - to transfer one's contract rights

to another. Contracts commonly assigned include leases, *mortgages*, and deeds of trust.

Auction Properties - A way of marketing property to the highest bidder. BIDS are taken verbally or simultaneously through mail or telegrams, and the property is sold to the highest bidder.

Authorized Borrower - Someone who is added on to another person's *revolving credit* account or *trade line*. An *authorized borrower* is authorized to use the account but does not share the same responsibilities as the primary holder of the account. The authorized borrower is not responsible for any bills and/or payments on the account.

B

Balloon Mortgage - A mortgage with a *balloon payment.*

   Example: The *balloon mortgage* called for payments of $500 per month for 5 years, followed by a BALLOON PAYMENT of $50,000.

Balloon Payment - The final payment on a loan, when that payment is greater than the previous installment payments and pays the loan in full.

Borrower - One who applies for and receives a loan in the form of a *mortgage* with the intention to repay.

Broker - A state-licensed agent who, for a fee, acts for property owners in real estate transactions

LEONARD "SPAR" PERSON JR.

Broker's Commission - The fee that a broker is paid after completing a real estate transaction

Buyer - The person purchasing the property

C

Certificate of Occupancy (C of O) - A document issued by a local government to a developer permitting the structure to be occupied by members of the public. Issuance of the certificate generally indicates that the building is in compliance with public health and building codes

Clause - A stipulation within a contract.

Closing - The act of transferring ownership of a property from *seller* to *buyer* in accordance with a sales contract

Closing Costs- Various fees and expenses paid by the seller and/or buyer at the time of a real estate closing

> **Example:** The following are some *closing costs*:

- Broker's Commission
- *Lender Rebate/*Discount Points, other fees
- *Title Insurance* premium
- Deed recording fees
- Loan *Prepayment Penalty*
- Inspection and *appraisal* fees
- Attorney Fees

Commercial Unit - property designed for use by retail, wholesale, office, hotel, or service users

Contract - An agreement between competent parties to do or not to do certain things for a consideration

LEONARD "SPAR" PERSON JR.

Contractor - one who is hired to supply specific goods or services, usually in connection with the development of a property

Counteroffer - When an *offer* is rejected, then a substitute offer is immediately proposed

Credit - one is granted a loan to buy now and pay later under designated terms based on a consumer's promise, ability, and track record of repaying; availability of money

Credit Delete Letter - A letter stating that the negative account will be removed from your *Credit Report* after the debt is paid or settled with the *creditor*

Credit Limit - The maximum amount of credit a lender

will extend to you on a particular account

Credit Report - A consumer's credit history evaluated by a credit bureau, including both credit and personal information about the consumer

Creditor - A business or person who extends credit or lends money to individuals or businesses; one who is owed money

    Example: *Creditors* include:

- Mortgage lenders
- Credit card companies (Macy's, American Express, etc.)
- Bond holders
- Loan companies

D

Debt - An obligation to pay

    Example: Kathy borrows $1000 from Rachel and therefore incurs a *debt*.

Debt-to-Income Ratio - Measures your future monthly housing expenses, which include your proposed mortgage payment (debt), property tax, and insurance in relation to your monthly income. Mortgage lenders generally figure that you shouldn't spend more than about 33 to 40 percent of your monthly income on housing expenses.

Deed - A legal document with which title to real property is transferred from one owner to another; Proof of ownership of a property.

Deed Transfer - The process of transferring ownership of a property from one person to another through the submission of legal documentation

Derogatory - Having a negative affect

Discount Points - See *lender rebate*

Down Payment - The part of the purchase price that the buyer pays in cash, up front, and does not finance with a mortgage

E

Equity - The difference between the *market value* of a home and the amount the borrower owes on it

> **Example:** If your home is worth $500,000 and your current outstanding mortgage is $300,000, your

equity is $200,000.

Escrow - The holding of important documents and money related to the purchase/sale of real estate by a neutral third party for safekeeping, pending the completion or performance of a specified act or condition

Example: The seller and the buyer come to an agreement that a leak on the boiler would be repaired prior to the closing date. Now they're at the closing and upon previously viewing the property the buyer realizes that the leak hasn't been repaired. The seller can either pay the $1000 upfront for the repair or hold $1000 in *escrow* for the specified amount of time. Within the specified time frame the seller either repairs the leak or loses the money in *escrow* to the buyer.

Escrow Account - A separate bank account in which the escrow officer (broker, attorney, etc.) is required by state law to deposit all monies collected for clients

F

Fair Credit Reporting Act (FCRA) - A federal law that allows individuals to examine and correct information used by *credit* reporting services.

    Example: Mary applies for a Macy's credit card. Macy's refuses to extend Mary any credit because of her poor credit rating. Under the Fair Credit Report Act, Mary may demand disclosure of Macy's source of information and then take steps to correct any incorrect details in the report.

Federal Housing Administration (FHA) - A federal agency within the Department of Housing and Urban

Development (HUD) which insures residential mortgage loans made by private lenders and sets standards for underwriting mortgage loans.

Fico (Fair Isaac Company) Score - A three digit number ranging from 350 - 850 devised by Fair Isaac, Inc., to measure a consumer's level of credit risk and based on information in the consumer's credit report

Fixed Rate - An interest rate that stays the same for the term of the loan

Fixed Rate Mortgage - A mortgage that allows you to lock in an *interest rate* for the entire term (generally 15 or 30 years) of the mortgage

Food Voucher - A document that that can be exchanged for food in place of money

LEONARD "SPAR" PERSON JR.

Foreclosure - The legal process by which a lender takes possession of and sells/auctions property in an attempt to pay off a mortgage loan that is in default

Foreclosure Sale - The process of paying the owner's debt (back mortgage payments he/she owes) and gaining possession of a property before the bank retains ownership of the property and it placed in an auction.

G

Good Faith Estimate - a written estimate of closing costs that the borrower will likely have to pay at closing. Since the actual costs are not known at the time, these estimates are based on *good faith,* or the lender's best estimate

Grace Period - The period of time during which a loan payment may be made after its due date without incurring a late fee/penalty. The *grace period* is specified within the terms of the loan and varies depending on the lender.

Example: Jack's American Express credit card payment I due on the 5th of the month. AMEX has a 5 day grace period with their credit cards. Jack doesn't make a payment until the 9th of the month. Because of AMEX's *grace period* the payment is not considered late and will not incur a late fee. Jack's payment will only be considered late after the 5 day grace period which would be anytime after the 10th day of the month.

H

Home Daycare - Daytime supervision and recreational,

LEONARD "SPAR" PERSON JR.

training, or medical facilities within a home for preschool children, physically challenged people, or seniors wishing special assistance

Home Equity Line of Credit - A type of Home Equity Loan that establishes an account that the borrower can withdraw money from, as desired. Interest accrues based on the amount of money actually borrowed, not the amount of the credit line.

   Example: Charles sets up a *Home Equity Line of Credit* at his bank. The Home Equity Line of Credit amount is $200,000. Charles withdraws $30,000 from the account. He will only be responsible for paying interest on the $30,000 he withdrew and not on the total $200,000.

P.S. In order for your home to qualify for a Home Equity Line of Credit, you must actually have *equity* in your home. Your line of credit amount can only be the amount of equity that is presently in your home or less.

Housing Urban Development (HUD) - The U.S. government department established to implement federal housing and community development programs. HUD oversees the Federal Housing Administration.

HUD 1 - A standard form that is prepared by whoever handles a *closing*. It contains itemized closing costs associated with purchasing/selling a home or refinancing a loan, and must be given to the buyer and seller.

I

Inquiry - A request from a potential creditor, employer, landlord, insurer to view an individual's credit report. An inquiry is listed on your credit report every time your credit report is pulled.

Inspection - a physical scrutinizing review of property or of documents

   Example: *Inspections* may be required for the following purposes:

- Sale requirements as to property conditions, such as wood-destroying insects (termites, etc.) or structural soundness
- Compliance with building codes
- Legal review of documents such as *leases* and *mortgages* to determine whether they are as they should be

Insurance - a coverage that protects you as a buyer from hazardous damages that may occur when owning a property

LEONARD "SPAR" PERSON JR.

Example: These are some hazardous damages that may be covered by your *insurance*:

- Fires
- Hurricanes
- Tornados
- Floods
- Vandalism to your property and/or robberies
- Jewelry, furniture and certain clothes such as Fur coats

Interest - A charge paid for borrowing money

Example: Banks/Lenders require payment of *interest* at a specified rate, to compensate for risk, deferment of benefits, inflation, and administrative burdens.

Interest Only Loan - A loan in which interest is payable at regular intervals until loan maturity, when the full loan balance is due.

    Example: A home was bought with a 5-year *interest only loan* of $100,000 at 8%. The *interest* of $8,000 was paid annually for 4 years. The $100,000 *principal*, together with the last $8,000 interest payment, was due at the end of the fifth year.

Interest Rate - A percentage of the amount borrowed. (Interest is the amount banks/lenders charge you to use their money)

Investment Property - a property that is purchased/owned for income production and capital growth potential, rather than for occupancy or use in a business. An *investment property* is usually for cash flow purposes and profitability.

Investor - A person or company that purchases

properties with the intentions to renovate and then resell it.

J

Joint Account Holder - one who is added to someone else's account and the liability shared among two or more people, each of whom is liable for the full debt.

Judgment - An official decision of a court stating that a debt is valid and orders payment. A *judgment* is a public record and is listed on your credit report as a negative or *derogatory* item.

      Example: These are some judgments that may appear on your credit report:

- Deferred leased car payments
- Unsettled lawsuits against you
- Unpaid IRS bills

LEONARD "SPAR" PERSON JR.

L

Lender - The bank, mortgage company, or mortgage broker offering the loan

Lender Rebate- An up-front fee paid to the lender which lowers your interest according to how many points are purchased. Each point equals 1% of the total loan amount.

    Example: At the time of Charles' loan application his offered rate is 8%. In order to get his rate lowered he would buy his rate down with a *lender rebate/discount points*. His loan amount is $100,000. He buys 2 points (each point equaling 1% of the *principal*) which amounts to $2,000. The $2,000 also applies to the loan amount, so the loan amount is now $98,000.

Letter of Authorization - A letter from the mortgagor (home owner that's responsible for the mortgage) stating that he/she gives the bank permission to discuss his/her loan details with a particular person. Letter of Authorizations are usually used when a property is in the process of being foreclosed and the home owner wants to try and conduct a *short sale* before he/she loses the property. A broker will require a *Letter of Authorization* in order to contact the bank and proceed with the short sale.

Lien - a legal claim against real or personal property for the purpose of satisfying a debt. A *lien* is security for the payment of a *debt, judgment*

Loan-to-Value (LTV) - The portion of the loan amount borrowed compared to the cost or value of the property purchased.

Example: Karen wants to purchase a 2 family home for $500,000. The *lender* that finances her the loan only lends a maximum of 95% LTV. If she qualifies for the 95% LTV, her loan amount will be $475,000 (95% of $500,000{the purchase price}). She will be responsible for paying the other 5% ($25,000) as a down payment.

Loss Mitigation Department - a department within the bank/lending institution, that deals with the loans that are in default or in the process of foreclosure.

M

Market Rate - The lowest commercial *interest rate* charged by banks on short-term loans to their most creditworthy customers. It is also known as the prime rate

Market Value - The theoretical highest price a buyer, willing but not compelled to buy, would pay, and the lowest price a seller, willing but not compelled to sell, would accept.

Example: An *appraisal* of a home indicates its *market value* is $400,000. In a normally active market, the home should sell for this amount if allowed to stay on the market for a reasonable time. The owner may, however, grow impatient and sell for $360,000 or may find an anxious buyer who will pay the $400,000.

Mix-Use Property - A property that consists of dwellings and a storefront.

Money Voucher - A document that can be exchanged for money.

Mortgage Broker - One who, for a fee, arranges

financing for borrowers, but does not service such loans. A *mortgage broker* works as an intermediary between the lender and the borrower.

Mortgage Broker's Fee - The fee that a *mortgage broker* is paid after a closing, for placing the loan.

Mortgage Taxes - A tax that has to be paid by the buyer to cover taxes charged to the mortgage broker.

Multi-Unit Property - A type of residential property with more than one dwelling unit in the same building.

    Example: Multi-Unit properties are divides into 2 categories:

- 2-4 dwelling units: duplexes, triplexes, and quadruplexes
- 5 or more units: apartment buildings

LEONARD "SPAR" PERSON JR.

N

No Point - No Fee Program - When a property is refinanced and the property owner does not pay any closing costs from his/her pockets. The fees are paid by the lenders rebate/points.

O

Occupancies - See *tenants.*

Occupied Sale - When a property is sold with tenant(s) occupying the premises. The property is not vacant.

Offer - An expression of willingness to purchase a property at a specified price or of willingness to sell. In real estate an offer is made by either party to the

LEONARD "SPAR" PERSON JR.

other.

    Example: Lincoln places his property on the market for $450,000. Adam makes an *offer* for $430,000. Lincoln may accept the offer, reject the offer, or propose a *counteroffer*.

Offer Sheet - a form that is filled out and sent to the real estate to place an *offer* on a property,

Option ARM Loan - See *Adjustable-Rate Mortgage (ARM)*

Overdraft - The amount that an account holder owes a bank because the balance in the account does not cover the amount that he or she has withdrawn from or debited to it

P

Payoff (Amount) - The remaining amount of a loan, including any prepayment penalty

Points - Fees paid to induce lenders to make a mortgage loan

Pre-approval - The process of determining how much money a prospective home buyer or refinancer will be eligible to borrow. The *pre-approval* is based upon thorough review of your financial situation

> **Example:** Jane wants to see a property listed with Heaven Homes Real Estate. The sales agent tells her that they require a *pre-approval* in order to show the property, so that they can make sure Jane will be able to get mortgage funding. Some real estates do that so that they are not showing their properties in

vein, to people that will not even be able to get financing for the homes.

Prepayment Penalty - A fee that is charged if the loan is paid off earlier than the specified term of the loan

Example: Linda borrowed $200,000 last year at 6% interest on a 30-year mortgage. The terms of her loan stated that she had a 3 year prepayment penalty of 5%. Now, one year later, she decides that she wants to sell her property. Because she is selling her property before the 30-year loan term, she is required to pay a *prepayment penalty* that amounts to $10,000. (P.S. if she would have sold it after owning it for 3 years she wouldn't have to pay the prepayment penalty because the term of the prepayment penalty was for 3 years). Some lenders do 1, 2, and 3 year prepayment penalties. If you are applying for a loan make sure that you DO NOT have a prepayment penalty.

LEONARD "SPAR" PERSON JR.

Prime Rate - See *market rate*

Principal - The amount of debt that is left on a loan (the balance), not including the interest

    Example: Frank arranged a loan of $100,000 at 6% *interest rate.* The monthly payment is $1,200 including $500 interest and $700 *principal.* The principal is what's going towards paying of the loan amount. The interest is what's going towards paying the bank fees. So after your first payment, you now owe $99,300 ($100,000 - $700)

Private Mortgage Insurance (PMI) - Insurance that protects the *lender* in case a borrower defaults on a mortgage

    Example: Ashley wishes to obtain a home purchase loan covering 90% of the value (90% *LTV).* The lender requires Ashley to acquire *Private Mortgage*

Insurance (PMI) as a condition for granting any loan for more than 80% of the value (80% LTV).

Property Tax - Yearly tax (paid by the owner) assessed on a home by the local government. Property taxes are based on a yearly basis, but can be broken down and paid quarterly (every 3 months) or can be included in your monthly mortgage payment.

Q

Quick Flip - When a property is bought for *under market value* and resold for *market value* in less than a year

R

Real Property - Land and any buildings such as homes,

garages, barns, tool sheds, or other structures permanently attached to the land

Redemption Period - The period during which any former owner can reclaim *foreclosed* property

Example: Carl's property was foreclosed. If he acts within his states *redemption period,* he can reclaim his property by paying the *debt* and legal fees.

Refinance - The process of paying off an old loan(s) with the proceeds of a new loan(s). People usually *refinance* for 2 reasons:

- To get a better *interest rate*
- To take cash out from the *equity* in their home

Renovation Sale - A property that has been fully renovated before being put on the market for sale

Example: A *renovation sale* consists of:

- New kitchen
- New bathroom
- New cosmetic work
- New appliances

Revolving Credit - A type of credit account that makes available a predetermined amount of money that can be used at any time without additional approval

S

Section 8 - A government rental program that helps assist low income families with their housing expenses

Secure Credit Line - A line of credit that is backed by real property such as a home, auto, boat, or securities

Seller's Concession - When the seller pays a

percentage towards the buyer's *closing costs*. It's usually between 3% - 6% depending on the bank.

(P.S. The *seller* has to agree to a *seller's concession*.)

Settlement (pertaining to Credit) - When a creditor is willing to settle for less that the original amount of a debt, usually one that's in collection, in order to receive some type of reimbursement for an unpaid loan

Settlement Letter - A letter from a *creditor* stating that you have settled/paid a debt that was owed to them

Short Sale - When a bank allows a broker to attempt to sell a property that is in the process of be foreclosed and auctioned. A property that is sold in a short sale is usually sold for less than what the owner paid for it

LEONARD "SPAR" PERSON JR.

Single Room Occupancy - A property that registered with the state, to only occupy single room rentals

Stated Loan - A loan that requires NO documents in order to be financed

Sub-prime Bank - A bank that offers loans to applicants with less-than-top-quality credit ratings (Sometimes referred to as "B-C lending"). These loans usually carry higher *interest rates* and a lower maximum *Loan-To-Value (LTV)*

Subsidized Housing - Apartments, nursing homes, or single-family dwellings that receive a government subsidy

T

Tax Certificate - A *tax lien* that can be bought at a government auction. When a *tax certificate* is bought, the property owner becomes indebted to the buyer.

Tax Deductible - A type of expense that is allowed under tax law, and can be used to reduce taxable income

    Example: These are a few things that are considered *tax deductible* when it comes to real estate:

- Interest paid on a mortgage
- Taxes paid on a property
- Repairs, maintenance, utilities, and other ordinary and necessary expenses are *tax deductible* for an *Investment Property.*

Tax Lien - A claim against a property for unpaid taxes

LEONARD "SPAR" PERSON JR.

Tenant - One who rents or leases real estate for a fixed period of time

Term Time - In a mortgage plan, the amount of time (typically 15 or 30 years) a lender gives a borrower to repay the loan

Title - A document that gives evidence of ownership of a property. The title also indicates the rights of ownership and possession of the property. Individuals who will have legal ownership in the property are considered "on title" and will sign the mortgage and other documentation.

Title Company - One in the business of examining *title* to real estate and/or issuing *title insurance.*

Title Fees - The fees and costs associated with a title

search and title insurance.

Title Insurance - Insurance that protects a lender against any title dispute that may arise over a particular property

Title Search - An examination of local real estate records to ensure that the seller is the legal owner of a property and that there are no liens or other claims against the property.

Trade Line - The different credit accounts listed on a borrower's credit report.

Example: These are examples of Trade Lines:
- Credit cards
- Bank loans
- Mortgages
- Or any number of other credit accounts

LEONARD "SPAR" PERSON JR.

Transfer Taxes - A tax paid when title passes from one owner to another. The *transfer taxes* are usually paid by the seller, unless other arrangements are discussed prior to *closing*.

U

Under Market Value - When a property is on the market for sale or has been sold for a price lower than its current market value/appraised value. A home *under market value* will have a good amount of equity in it.

Example: Sue's aunt Mrs. Smith is selling her 2 family brownstone in Clinton Hills, Brooklyn, NY. Now, normally a 2 family brownstone in Clinton Hills would sell anywhere from $800,000 to $1.5 million, but since Sue is Mrs. Smith's niece, she is willing to sell her the property for $600,000 (which is a steal!). Sue, now acquires a property for *under market value*, and in addition has a substantial amount of equity in the property.

V

Vacant Sale - When a property is sold without any tenants or occupancies of the premises. The property is vacant.

Verification of Deposit (VOD) - A document signed by the borrower's bank or other financial institution verifying the borrower's account balance and history

Verification of Employment (VOE) - A document signed by the borrower's employer verifying the borrower's position and salary

Verification of Rent (VOR) or Mortgage (VOM) - A

document used to verify the mortgage or rent history of a borrower

100% Financing - When one acquires a loan for the total amount of the purchase price, without having to pay a down payment for a property

80/20 - A loan in which a first mortgage covering 80% of the value of the home is combined with a second mortgage that covers the remaining 20%

LEONARD "SPAR" PERSON JR.

INDEX

LEONARD "SPAR" PERSON JR.

Under market value, 113

Vacant sale, 106

Working people rentals, 93

LEONARD "SPAR" PERSON JR.

CONTACTS

HOOD ESTATE, LLC

(718) 775-9057 office

(800) 699-7020 Toll free

www.hoodestate.com

HEAVEN HOMES, LLC

(718) 775-9086 office

(877) 233-0148 fax

EQUIFAX (Credit Bureau)

Equifax

P.O.Box740241

Atlanta, GA 30374

www.equifax.com - to dispute your accounts online

1-800-685-1111 customer service

1-888-766-0008 to place a Fraud Alert on your credit

LEONARD "SPAR" PERSON JR.

report

EXPERIAN (Credit Bureau)

Experian

P.O. Box 2002

Allen, TX 75013

www.experian.com/reportaccess - to dispute your accounts online

1-888-397-3742 customer service or to place a Fraud Alert on your credit report

TRANSUNION (Credit Bureau)

TransUnion

P.O. Box 1000

Chester, PA 19022

www.transunion.com - to dispute your accounts online

1-800-916-8800 to dispute your accounts by phone

1-800-888-4213 customer service

LEONARD "SPAR" PERSON JR.

1-800-680-7289 to place a Fraud Alert on your credit
report

PROPERTY SHARK

Property Research Partners LLC

181 N. 11th Street, Suite 307

Brooklyn, NY 11211

www.propertyshark.com

Customer service:

(718) 715-1758

(213) 291-8576

(415) 839-8694

ZILLOW

999 Third Ave

Suite 4600

Seattle, WA 98104

www.zillow.com

LEONARD "SPAR" PERSON JR.

HOOD ESTATE DIAGRAMS

You can view a copy of an Appraisal, Title Search, 1003 Application, Residential Contract of Sale and Credit Report Diagrams on the Hood Estate CD that comes with this book.

www.Hoodestate.com

1-800-699-7020

LEONARD "SPAR" PERSON JR.

Request for Verification of Deposit

Privacy Act Notice: This information is to be used by the agency collecting it or its assignees in determining whether you qualify as a prospective mortgagor under its program. It will not be disclosed outside the agency except as required and permitted by law. You do not have to provide this information, but if you do not your application for approval as a prospective mortgagor or borrower may be delayed or rejected. The information requested in this form is authorized by Title 38, USC, Chapter 37 (if VA); by 12 USC, Section 1701 et. seq. (if HUD/FHA), by 42 USC, Section 1452b (if HUD/CPD); and Title 42 USC, 1471 et. seq., or 7 USC, 1921 et. seq. (if USDA/FmHA).

Instructions: Lender - Complete items 1 through 8. Have applicant complete item 9. Forward directly to depository named in item 1.
Depository - Please complete items 10 through 18 and return directly to lender named in item 2.
The form is to be transmitted directly to the lender and is not to be transmitted through the applicant(s) or any other party.

Lender's Phone No.
718-555-5555

Part I - Request

1. To (Name and address of depository)

2. From (Name and address of lender)

HOOD ESTATE
555 HOOD ESTATE AVE
BROOKLYN, NY 11217

I certify that this verification has been sent directly to the bank or depository and has not passed through the hands of the applicant or any other interested party.

3. Signature of Lender	4. Title	5. Date	6. Lender's No. (Optional)

7. Information To Be Verified

Type of Account	Account in Name of	Account Number	Balance
			$
			$
			$
			$

To Depository: I/We have applied for a mortgage loan and stated in my/our financial statement that the balance on deposit with you is as shown above. You are authorized to verify this information and to supply the lender identified above with the information requested in items 10 through 13. Your response is solely a matter of courtesy for which no responsibility is attached to your institution or any of your officers.

8. Name and Address of Applicant(s)	9. Signature of Applicant(s)
	X
	X

To Be Completed by Depository

Part II - Verification of Depository

10. Deposit Accounts of Applicant(s)

Type of Account	Account Number	Current Balance	Average Balance For Previous Two Months	Date Opened
		$	$	
		$	$	
		$	$	
		$	$	

11. Loans Outstanding To Applicant(s)

Loan Number	Date of Loan	Original Amount	Current Balance	Installments	(Monthly/Quarterly)	Secured By	No. of Late Payments
		$	$	$	per		
		$	$	$	per		
		$	$	$	per		

12. Please include any additional information which may be of assistance in determination of credit worthiness (Please include information on loans paid-in full in item 11 above.)

13. If the name(s) on the account(s) differ from those listed in item 7, please supply the name(s) on the account(s) as reflected by your records.

Part III - Authorized Signature

Federal statutes provide severe penalties for any fraud, intentional misrepresentation, or criminal connivance or conspiracy purposed to influence the issuance of any guaranty or insurance by the VA Secretary, the U.S.D.A., FmHA/FHA Commisioner, or the HUD/CPD Assistant Secretary.

14. Signature of Depository Representative	15. Title (Please print or type)	16. Date
17. Please print or type name signed in item 14	18. Phone No.	

CALYX Form vod.frm 12/96

LEONARD "SPAR" PERSON JR.

REQUEST FOR VERIFICATION OF RENT OR MORTGAGE

We have received an application for a loan from the applicant listed below, to whom we understand you rent or have extended a loan.

INSTRUCTIONS: LENDER - Complete items 1 thru 8. Have applicant(s) complete item 9. Forward directly to lender named in Item 1.
LANDLORD/CREDITOR - Please complete Part II as applicable. Sign and return directly to the lender named in Item 2.

PART I - REQUEST

1. TO (Name and address of Landlord/Creditor)	2. FROM (Name and address of lender)
	HOOD ESTATE 555 HOOD ESTATE AVE BROOKLYN, NY 11217

3. SIGNATURE OF LENDER	4. TITLE	5. DATE	6. LENDER'S NUMBER

7. INFORMATION TO BE VERIFIED.

☐ MORTGAGE ☐ LAND CONTRACT ☐ RENTAL ☐	PROPERTY ADDRESS	ACCOUNT IN THE NAME OF:	ACCOUNT NO.

8. NAME AND ADDRESS OF APPLICANT(S)	9. SIGNATURE OF APPLICANT(S)

PART II - TO BE COMPLETED BY LANDLORD/CREDITOR

☐ RENTAL ACCOUNT	☐ MORTGAGE ACCOUNT ☐ LAND CONTRACT
Tenant has rented since _____	Date mortgage originated _____ Interest rate _____
to _____	Original mortgage amount $_____ FIXED _____ ARM _____
Amount of rent $_____ per _____	Current mortgage balance $_____ FHA _____ VA _____
Is rent in arrears? Yes _____ No _____	Monthly Payment P & I only $_____ FNMA _____ CONV _____
Amount $ _____ Period _____	Payment with taxes & ins. $_____ Next pay date _____
Number of times 30 days past due* _____	Is mortgage current? Yes _____ No _____ No of late payments*_____
Is account satisfactory? Yes _____ No _____	Is mortgage assumable? Yes _____ No _____ Insurance agent: _____
_____	Satisfactory account? Yes _____ No _____ _____
	* Number of times account has been 30 days overdue in last 12 months

ADDITIONAL INFORMATION WHICH MAY BE OF ASSISTANCE IN DETERMINING APPLICANT(S) CREDIT WORTHINESS

SIGNATURE OF CREDITOR	TITLE	DATE
	PHONE NO.	

The confidentiality of the information you have furnished will be preserved except where disclosure of this information is required by applicable law. The form is to be transmitted directly to the lender and is not to be transmitted through the applicant or any other party.

Calyx Form Vom.frm 5/97

LEONARD "SPAR" PERSON JR.

Request for Verification of Employment

Privacy Act Notice: This information is to be used by the agency collecting it or its assignees in determining whether you qualify as a prospective mortgagor under its program. It will not be disclosed outside the agency except as required and permitted by law. You do not have to provide this information, but if you do not your application for approval as a prospective mortgagor or borrower may be delayed or rejected. The information requested in this form is authorized by Title 38, USC, Chapter 37 (if VA); by 12 USC, Section 1701 et seq. (if HUD/FHA); by 42 USC, Section 1452b (if HUD/CPD); and Title 42 USC, 1471 et. seq., or 7 USC, 1921 et. seq. (if USDA/FmHA).

Instructions: Lender - Complete items 1 through 7. Have applicant complete item 8. Forward directly to employer, named in item 1.
Employer - Please complete either Part II or Part III as applicable. Complete Part IV and return directly to lender named in item 2.
The form is to be transmitted directly to the lender and is not to be transmitted through the applicant or any other party.

Part I - Request

1. To (Name and address of employer)	2. From (Name and address of lender)
	HOOD ESTATE
	555 HOOD ESTATE AVE
	BROOKLYN, NY 11217

I certify that this verification has been sent directly to the employer and has not passed through the hands of the applicant or any other interested party.

3. Signature of Lender	4. Title	5. Date	6. Lender's No. (Optional)

I have applied for a mortgage loan and stated that I am now or was formerly employed by you. My signature below authorizes verification of this information.

7. Name and Address of Applicant (include employee or badge number)	8. Signature of Applicant

Part II - Verification of Present Employment

9. Applicant's Date of Employment	10. Present Position	11. Probability of Continued Employment

12A. Current **Gross Base Pay** (Enter Amount and Check Period)		13. For Military Personnel Only		14. If Overtime or Bonus is Applicable, Is Its Continuance Likely?
☐ Annual ☐ Hourly		Pay Grade		Overtime Yes ☐ No ☐
☐ Monthly ☐ Other (Specify)		Type	Monthly Amount	Bonus Yes ☐ No ☐
$ ☐ Weekly		Base Pay	$	15. If paid hourly-average hours per week

12B. Gross Earnings

Type	Year To Date	Past Year ___	Past Year ___	Rations	$	
	Thru ___			Flight or	$	16. Date of applicant's next pay increase
Base Pay	$	$	$	Hazard		
				Clothing	$	
Overtime	$	$	$	Quarters	$	17. Projected amount of next pay increase
Commissions	$	$	$	Pro Pay	$	18. Date of applicant's last pay increase
				Overseas or	$	
Bonus	$	$	$	Combat		19. Amount of last pay increase
				Variable Housing	$	
Total	$	$	$	Allowance		

20. Remarks (if employee was off work for any length of time, please indicate time period and reason)

Part III - Verification of Previous Employments

21. Date Hired	23. Salary/Wage at Termination Per (Year)(Month)(Week)			
22. Date Terminated	Base	Overtime	Commissions	Bonus
24. Reason for Leaving		25. Position Held		

Part IV - Authorized Signature

Federal statutes provide severe penalties for any fraud, intentional misrepresentation, or criminal connivance or conspiracy purposed to influence the issuance of any guaranty or insurance by the VA Secretary, the U.S.D.A., FmHA/FHA Commissioner, or the HUD/CPD Assistant Secretary.

26. Signature of Employer	27. Title (Please print or type)	28. Date
29. Print or type name signed in Item 26	30. Phone No.	

CALYX Form voe.frm 5/97

LEONARD "SPAR" PERSON JR.

Commencement Date: _____   Security Deposit: $ _____

Termination Date: _____

1. Use and Occupancy
The Unit may only be used strictly for residential purposes and may only be occupied by Tenant and Tenant's spouse and children.

2. Inability to Give Possession
The failure of Landlord to give Tenant possession of the Unit on the Commencement Date shall not create liability for Landlord. In the event that possession of the Unit is not delivered on the Commencement Date, Monthly Rent hereunder shall begin on the date that possession of the Unit is delivered to Tenant and shall be prorated for that portion of the month in which possession is delivered.

3. Rent
Tenant shall pay Monthly Rent in full on the first day of each month of the Lease. Monthly Rent shall be paid in advance with no notice being required from Landlord. Tenant shall not deduct any sums from the Monthly Rent unless Landlord consents thereto in writing.

Upon signing this Lease, Tenant shall pay Landlord the first Monthly Rent due and the Security Deposit. The entire amount of rent due for the Lease Term is due upon signing this Lease; however, Landlord consents to the Tenant paying same in monthly installments provided there exists no defaults by Tenant under the terms of this Lease.

Additional Rent may include, but is not limited to any additional insurance premiums and/or expenses paid by Landlord which are chargeable to Tenant as stated hereinafter. Additional Rent is due and payable with the Monthly Rent for the next month after Tenant receives notice form Landlord that Additional Rent is due and payable.

4. Condition of Unit
Tenant acknowledges that Tenant is accepting the Unit in its **"as is"** condition. Tenant further acknowledges that Tenant has thoroughly inspected the Unit and has found the Unit to be in good order and repair and that the appliances, if any, are in good operating condition. Tenant further states that Tenant knows how to operate the appliances and shall do so in accordance with the manufacturer's instructions.

5. Security
The Security Deposit is due upon the Tenant signing this Lease. The Security Deposit shall not be used for the payment of Monthly Rent unless agreed to, in writing, by Landlord and Tenant. Landlord shall deposit the Security Deposit in a bank insured by the FDIC and same will accrue interest if mandated by law. Within ten (10) days after Tenant surrenders possession of the Unit at the expiration of the Lease Term, Landlord shall return the Security Deposit, less any cost of repairs as authorized by this Lease, to Tenant at an address Tenant provides.

6. Services and Utilities
Tenant is responsible fro paying all electric, gas, water, telephone and any other utilities allocated to the Unit. Use of a dishwasher, clothes washer and dryer machines, freezer, air purifier, portable heater, air conditioner or similar appliances is prohibited without Landlord's written consent.

Landlord will supply (a) heat, in such quantity and for such time as mandated by law, (b) hot and cold water, (c) air conditioning, if already existing in the Unit, (d) garbage removal from the Premises (the "Services"). If the Services are temporarily interrupted due to an accident, emergency and/or repairs, Tenant's obligation to pay rent, in full, shall not be affected thereby.

Landlord will also supply a refrigerator, stove/oven, dishwasher, window air conditioning unit, clothes washer and clothes dryer (the "Appliances"). Any damage to the Appliances which is caused by the willful and/or negligent acts of Tenant may be repaired by Landlord, the cost of which shall be Additional Rent.

7. Furnishings
The Unit is being delivered (furnished) (unfurnished). If furnished, Landlord has given an inventory of the furnishings which inventory has been signed by Tenant and Landlord. Tenant acknowledges that said furnishings are in good condition and Tenant accepts same in **"as is"** condition.

8. Repairs and Alterations
Tenant shall maintain all appliances, equipment, furniture, furnishings and other personal property included under this Lease and, upon the surrender of the Unit on the Termination Date, Tenant shall surrender same to Landlord in the same condition as received, reasonable wear and tear excepted. Tenant shall make all repairs which become necessary due to Tenant's acts and/or negligence. If Tenant does not make such repairs, Landlord may do so, the cost of which shall be Additional Rent. In the event that Tenant defaults under the terms of this Paragraph 9, Landlord may make necessary repairs or replacement, the cost of which shall be deducted from the Security Deposit.

Tenant shall not make any alterations, additions, modifications and/or changes to the Unit during the Lease Term.

9. Maintenance of Unit
Tenant shall maintain the Unit in a neat, clean and presentable condition.

10. Pets
Pets of any kind or nature (shall) (shall not) be allowed in the Unit.

11. Damage, Fire or Other Catastrophe
In the case of fire damage or other damage to the Unit not caused by Tenant, Tenant shall give Landlord immediate notice of same. Upon receipt of such notice, Landlord may either (a) repair the Unit or (b) terminate

LEONARD "SPAR" PERSON JR.

Premises. Landlord may cancel this Lease, in such event, upon thirty (30) days written notice to Tenant of Landlord's intent, which notice shall include the date on which the Lease terminates, which shall, in no event, be less than thirty (30) days from the date of said notice. By canceling this Lease in accordance with the terms of this Paragraph, Landlord is not obligated to repair, renovate or rebuild the Premises. Monthly Rent and Additional Rent shall be paid by Tenant up to the date of the Occurrence.

12. Liability
Landlord shall not be liable for any loss, damage or expense to any person or property except if such loss is caused by the willful acts of Landlord.
Tenant shall be liable for the acts of Tenant, Tenant's family, guests and/or invitees. Landlord's cost and expense in repairing any such damage or from any claim resulting from such acts shall be billed as Additional Rent and shall be paid by Tenant to Landlord.

13. Landlord's Entry
Except in an emergency, for the purposes of repair, inspection, extermination, installation or repair of any system, utility or appliance or to do any work deemed necessary by Landlord, Landlord may enter the Unit on reasonable notice and at reasonable times. Upon giving such notice, Landlord may also enter the Unit to show the Unit to prospective purchasers, lenders or other persons deemed appropriate and necessary by Landlord. During the last three (3) months of the Term of this Lease, Landlord may enter the Unit to show the Unit to prospective tenants.

14. Assigning or Subletting
This Lease may not be assigned by Tenant nor shall Tenant sublet the Unit.

15. Subordination
This Lease and Tenant's rights hereunder are subject and subordinate to all existing and future leases for the land on which the Premises stand, to all mortgages on said leases and/or the Premises and/or the land and all renewals, modifications and extensions thereof. Upon request by Landlord, Tenant shall execute any certificate to this effect.

16. Landlord's Consent
If, under the terms of this Lease, the consent of Landlord is required, such consent shall not be unreasonably withheld.

17. Keys, Locks
Tenant shall give Landlord keys to all locks for the Unit. Tenant shall not change any locks or add any locks to the Unit without obtaining Landlord's consent, and if given, Tenant shall provide keys to Landlord for these locks.

18. Signs
Tenant shall not place any signs on the Premises or upon the grounds on which the Premises stand or in the Unit so as to be seen from outside the Unit.
Landlord shall have the right to place or cause to be placed on the Premises and/or upon the grounds on

2. a default under Paragraph 30 of this Lease, thirty (30) days.
B. In the event that Tenant fails to cure a default within the time stated therefore, Landlord may terminate this Lease. In such event, Landlord shall give Tenant notice stating the date upon which this Lease shall terminate, such date being not less than three (3) days after the date of such notice at which time this Lease shall then terminate. Tenant shall be responsible for Monthly Rent and Additional Rent as set forth in this Lease up to the date of termination.
C. If this Lease is terminated or Tenant vacates the Unit prior to the Termination Date, Landlord may enter the Unit and remove Tenant and any person or property and/or commence summary proceedings for eviction. The aforesaid actions are not the sole remedies of Landlord.
D. If this Lease is cancelled or Landlord takes back the Unit
1. Monthly Rent and Additional Rent for the unexpired portion of the Term immediately becomes due and payable. In addition, any cost or repair expended by Landlord shall be the obligation of Tenant and shall be deemed Additional Rent.
2. Landlord may re-rent the Unit and anything in it for any term and at any rental and any cost in connection therewith shall be borne by Tenant which may include, but is not limited to the cost of repairs, decorations, preparation for renting, broker's fees, advertising costs and attorney's fees. Any rent recovered by Landlord for the re-renting of the Unit shall reduce the amount of money that Tenant owes to Landlord.

21. Landlord's Rules
Tenant shall comply with these rules (the "Rules") at all times. If there is a change in the rules, Landlord will give Tenant notice of same. Landlord shall not be liable to Tenant for another Tenant's violation of the Rules. The rights afforded under the following Rules are for the sole benefit of Landlord:
(a) the quiet enjoyment of other tenants shall not be interfered with;
(b) sounds, odors and lights which are annoying to other tenants are not allowed;
(c) floors within the Unit must be covered over 70% of the area of each room except for the bathroom and kitchen;
(d) all posted rules must be followed;
(e) smoking is not permitted in the Unit or hallways;
(f) All flammable or dangerous items may not be kept or stored in the Unit;
(g) no one is allowed access to or the enjoyment of the roof;
(h) nothing shall be placed on or attached to the fire escapes, windows, doors or in the hallways or common areas;
(i) elevators, if any, are to be used by tenants and their guests only. Bicycles are not allowed in the elevators. Tenants and their guests are not to leave any garbage, trash and/or debris in the elevators;
(j) moving of furniture in and out of the Unit must be scheduled with the Landlord;
(k) all deliveries must be made by means of the service entrance, if any;
(l) laundry machines, if provided, may be used at tenants' risk and cost, may only be used at reasonable

196

LEONARD "SPAR" PERSON JR.

23. Limitation of Recovery
Should Tenant obtain a judgment or other remedy from a court of competent jurisdiction for the payment of money by Landlord, Tenant is limited to the Landlord's interest in the Premises for the collection of same.

24. Construction and Demolition
Construction and/or demolition may be done in or near the Premises and if same interferes with the ventilation, view and/or enjoyment of the Unit, Tenant's obligations under this Lease shall, in no way, be affected.

25. Demolition of Premises
Should Landlord deem it necessary to demolish the Premises, Landlord may terminate this Lease upon six (6) months written notice to Tenant provided such notice is given to all other tenants in the Premises. In such event, Tenant shall surrender the Unit to Landlord upon such date as set forth in the notice.

26. Terraces and Balconies
If there is a terrace or balcony as an adjunct to the Unit, such terrace or balcony is subject to the terms of this Lease.

Tenant shall keep the terrace or balcony clean, clear of snow, ice, garbage and other debris. No alteration or additions may be made to the terrace or balcony. Tenant's property may not be stored on the terrace or balcony. Cooking on the terrace or balcony is prohibited.

Tenant shall maintain the terrace or balcony in good condition and make all repairs at Tenant's cost, except those of a structural nature which is the responsibility of Landlord.

27. Common Recreational Areas
If applicable, Landlord may give Tenant use of any playground, pool, parking or other areas, the use of which will be at Tenant's own risk and Tenant shall pay any charge imposed by Landlord for such use. Landlord's permission to use these areas may be revoked at any time.

28. Landlord's Employees
The employees of Landlord shall not perform any work for Tenant at Tenant's request. Such employees may not do any personal chores of Tenant.

29. Condemnation
If any or part of the Premises is taken or condemned by any governmental authority, Landlord may cancel this Lease on notice to Tenant and Tenant's rights hereunder shall end as of the date the authority takes title to the Premises which cancellation date can not be less than thirty (30) days from the date of Landlord's notice. Tenant shall be liable for Monthly Rent and Additional Rent to the date of cancellation and shall make no claim for the unexpired term of the Lease. Any award for the condemnation is the property of Landlord and Tenant assigns to Landlord any and all rights, interest and/or claim in and to such award.

30. Bankruptcy
Should Tenant file a voluntary petition in bankruptcy or an involuntary petition is filed against Tenant, or should Tenant assign any property fro the benefit of

a summary proceeding for eviction, Tenant waives Tenant's right to any set-off and/or counterclaim.

33. Broker
Tenant states that _____ is the sole Broker who showed the Unit to Tenant. Tenant shall hold harmless and indemnify Landlord fro any monies expended by Landlord should Tenant's statement herein be untrue.

34. Inability of Landlord to Perform
If Landlord is unable to perform any of its obligations to be performed hereunder due to governmental orders, labor strife or inability to secure goods or materials, through no fault on the part of Landlord, this Lease shall not be terminated or cancelled and such inability shall not impact upon Tenant's obligations hereunder.

35. Illegality
Should any part of this Lease be deemed illegal, the remaining portions of this Lease shall not be affected thereby and shall remain in full force and effect.

36. Non-Disturbance
So long as Tenant pays the Monthly Rent and Additional Rent and there exists no defaults under any of the terms of this Lease, Tenant may peacefully occupy the Unit for the Lease Term.

37. Non-Waiver
Any failure by Landlord to insist upon Tenant's full compliance with the terms of this Lease and/or to enforce such terms shall not be deemed to be a waiver of Landlord's rights to insist upon or so enforce the terms of this Lease at a future date.

38. Parties Bound
This Lease is binding upon Landlord and Tenant and their respective assignees and/or successors in interest.

39. Paragraph Headings
Paragraph headings are for reference only.

40. Effectiveness
This Lease shall become effective as of the date when Landlord delivers a fully executed copy hereof to Tenant or Tenant's attorney.

41. Entire Agreement
Tenant states that Tenant has read this Lease and that it fully incorporates all understandings, representations and promises made to Tenant by Landlord and/or Landlord's agent and that this Lease supercedes all prior representations, agreements and promises, whether oral or written.

42. Amendments
This Lease may only be changed or amended in a writing signed by the parties hereto.

43. Riders
Additional terms are contained in the riders annexed hereto and designated Rider _____.

197

LEONARD "SPAR" PERSON JR.

Place of Settlement:	I. Settlement Date:

J. Summary of Borrower's Transaction		K. Summary of Seller's Transaction	
100. Gross Amount Due From Borrower		**400. Gross Amount Due To Seller**	
101. Contract sales price		401. Contract sales price	
102. Personal property		402. Personal property	
103. Settlement charges to borrower (line 1400)		403.	
104.		404.	
105.		405.	
Adjustments for items paid by seller in advance		**Adjustments for items paid by seller in advance**	
106. City/town taxes to		406. City/town taxes to	
107. County taxes to		407. County taxes to	
108. Assessments to		408. Assessments to	
109.		409.	
110.		410.	
111.		411.	
112.		412.	
120. Gross Amount Due From Borrower		**420. Gross Amount Due To Seller**	
200. Amounts Paid By Or In Behalf Of Borrower		**500. Reductions In Amount Due To Seller**	
201. Deposit or earnest money		501. Excess deposit (see instructions)	
202. Principal amount of new loan(s)		502. Settlement charges to seller (line 1400)	
203. Existing loan(s) taken subject to		503. Existing loan(s) taken subject to	
204.		504. Payoff of first mortgage loan	
205.		505. Payoff of second mortgage loan	
206.		506.	
207.		507.	
208.		508.	
209.		509.	
Adjustments for items unpaid by seller		**Adjustments for items unpaid by seller**	
210. City/town taxes to		510. City/town taxes to	
211. County taxes to		511. County taxes to	
212. Assessments to		512. Assessments to	
213.		513.	
214.		514.	
215.		515.	
216.		516.	
217.		517.	
218.		518.	
219.		519.	
220. Total Paid By/For Borrower		**520. Total Reduction Amount Due Seller**	
300. Cash At Settlement From/To Borrower		**600. Cash At Settlement To/From Seller**	
301. Gross Amount due from borrower (line 120)		601. Gross amount due to seller (line 420)	
302. Less amounts paid by/for borrower (line 220) (	)	602. Less reductions in amt. due seller (line 520) (	)
303. Cash ☐ From ☐ To Borrower		**603. Cash** ☐ To ☐ From Seller	

Section 5 of the Real Estate Settlement Procedures Act (RESPA) requires the following: • HUD must develop a Special Information Booklet to help persons borrowing money to finance the purchase of residential real estate to better understand the nature and costs of real estate settlement services; • Each lender must provide the booklet to all applicants from whom it receives or for whom it prepares a written application to borrow money to finance the purchase of residential real estate; • Lenders must prepare and distribute with the Booklet a Good Faith Estimate of the settlement costs that the borrower is likely to incur in connection with the settlement. These disclosures are manadatory.

Section 4(a) of RESPA mandates that HUD develop and prescribe this standard form to be used at the time of loan settlement to provide full disclosure of all charges imposed upon the borrower and seller. These are third party disclosures that are designed to provide the borrower with pertinent information during the settlement process in order to be a better shopper.

The Public Reporting Burden for this collection of information is estimated to average one hour per response, including the time for reviewing instructions, searching existing data sources, gathering and maintaining the data needed, and completing and reviewing the collection of information.

This agency may not collect this information, and you are not required to complete this form, unless it displays a currently valid OMB control number.

The information requested does not lend itself to confidentiality.

LEONARD "SPAR" PERSON JR.

~~.					
810.					
811.					
900.	**Items Required By Lender To Be Paid In Advance**				
901.	Interest from	to	@ $	/day	
902.	Mortgage Insurance Premium for			months to	
903.	Hazard Insurance Premium for			years to	
904.				years to	
905.					
1000.	**Reserves Deposited With Lender**				
1001.	Hazard insurance		months@$	per month	
1002.	Mortgage insurance		months@$	per month	
1003.	City property taxes		months@$	per month	
1004.	County property taxes		months@$	per month	
1005.	Annual assessments		months@$	per month	
1006.			months@$	per month	
1007.			months@$	per month	
1008.			months@$	per month	
1100.	**Title Charges**				
1101.	Settlement or closing fee		to		
1102.	Abstract or title search		to		
1103.	Title examination		to		
1104.	Title insurance binder		to		
1105.	Document preparation		to		
1106.	Notary fees		to		
1107.	Attorney's fees		to		
	(includes above items numbers:			)	
1108.	Title insurance		to		
	(includes above items numbers:			)	
1109.	Lender's coverage		$		
1110.	Owner's coverage		$		
1111.					
1112.					
1113.					
1200.	**Government Recording and Transfer Charges**				
1201.	Recording fees: Deed $	; Mortgage $	; Releases $		
1202.	City/county tax/stamps: Deed $	; Mortgage $			
1203.	State tax/stamps: Deed $	; Mortgage $			
1204.					
1205.					
1300.	**Additional Settlement Charges**				
1301.	Survey	to			
1302.	Pest inspection to				
1303.					
1304.					
1305.					
1400.	**Total Settlement Charges (enter on lines 103, Section J and 502, Section K)**				

LEONARD "SPAR" PERSON JR.

1242 HALSEY STREET, S/S 200'0" West of Knickerbocker Avenue

Block **3412** . Lot **24**

, conforms substantially to the approved plans and specifications, and to the requirements of the building code and all other laws and ordinances, and of the rules and regulations of the Board of Standards and Appeals, applicable to a building of its class and kind at the time the permit was issued; and

CERTIFIES FURTHER that, any provisions of Section 646F of the New York Charter have been complied with as certified by a report of the Fire Commissioner to the Borough Superintendent. **Brick**

~~KNICKERBOCKE~~ Alt. 3945/1946 Construction classification— **Non-fireproof**

Occupancy classification— **Converted Dwelling** . Height **2 & Base,** stories. **25** feet.
Class 'A'

Date of completion— **Const. 5-14-54** Located in **Residence** Use District.
C **Plumb. 5-14-5**
H.D. 5-20-54 Area Height Zone at time of issuance of permit

This certificate is issued subject to the limitations hereinafter specified and to the following resolutions of the Board of Standards and Appeals: (Calendar numbers to be inserted here)

PERMISSIBLE USE AND OCCUPANCY

STORY	LIVE LOADS lbs. per Sq. Ft.	PERSONS ACCOMMODATED			USE
		MALE	FEMALE	TOTAL	
CELLAR	GROUND	--	--	--	Ordinary
BASEMENT	40	--	--	--	One (1) family
First	40	--	--	--	One (1 family
Second	40	--	--	--	One (1) family

TOTAL - Three (3) families

Class 'A' Multiple Dwelling - Converted

(Complies with Section 264 Multiple Dwelling Law)

Borough Superintendent

CERTIFICATE WILL BE NULL AND VOID IF ALTERED IN ANY MANNER OR ADDITIONS ARE MADE THERETO.
(Page 1)

200

be any reduction or diminution of the area of the lot or plot on which the building is located.

The building or any part thereof shall not be used for any purpose other than that for which it is certified.

The superimposed, uniformly distributed loads, or concentrated loads producing the same stresses in the construction in any story shall not exceed the live loads specified on reverse side; the number of persons of either sex in any story shall not exceed that specified when sex is indicated, nor shall the aggregate number of persons in any story exceed the specified total; and the use to which any story may be put shall be restricted to that fixed by this certificate except as specifically stated.

This certificate does not in any way relieve the owner or owners or any other person or persons in possession or control of the building, or any part thereof from obtaining such other permits, licenses or approvals as may be prescribed by law for the uses or purposes for which the building is designed or intended; nor from obtaining the special certificates required for the use and operation of elevators; nor from the installation of fire alarm systems where required by law; nor from complying with any lawful order for additional fire extinguishing appliances under the discretionary powers of the fire commissioner; nor from complying with any lawful order issued with the object of maintaining the building in a safe or lawful condition; nor from complying with any authorized direction to remove encroachments into a public highway or other public place, whether attached to or part of the building or not.

If this certificate is marked "Temporary", it is applicable only to those parts of the building indicated on its face, and certifies to the legal use and occupancy of only such parts of the building; it is subject to all the provisions and conditions applying to a final or permanent certificate; it is not applicable to any building under the jurisdiction of the Housing Division unless it is also approved and endorsed by them, and it must be replaced by a full certificate at the date of expiration.

If this certificate is for an existing building, erected prior to March 14, 1916, it has been duly inspected and it has been found to have been occupied or arranged to be occupied prior to March 14, 1916, as noted on the reverse side, and that on information and belief, since that date there has been no alteration or conversion to a use that changed its classification as defined in the Building Code, or that would necessitate compliance with some special requirement or with the State Labor Law or any other law or ordinance; that there are no notices of violations or orders pending in the Department of Housing and Buildings at this time; that Section 646F of the New York City Charter has been complied with as certified by a report of the Fire Commissioner to the Borough Superintendent, and that, so long as the building is not altered, except by permission of the Borough Superintendent, the existing use and occupancy may be continued.

"§ 646 F. No certificate of occupancy shall be issued for any building, structure, enclosure, place or premises wherein containers for combustibles, chemicals, explosives, inflammables and other dangerous substances, articles, compounds or mixtures are stored, or wherein automatic or other fire alarm systems or fire extinguishing equipment are required by law to be or are installed, until the fire commissioner has tested and inspected and has certified his approval in writing of the installation of such containers, systems or equipment to the Borough Superintendent of the borough in which the installation has been made. Such approval shall be recorded on the certificate of occupancy."

Additional copies of this certificate will be furnished to persons having an interest in the building or premises, upon payment of a fee of fifty cents per copy.

BARGAIN AND SALE DEED WITH COVENANT AGAINST GRANTOR'S ACTS (INDIVIDUAL OR CORPORATION)

FORM 8007

CAUTION: THIS AGREEMENT SHOULD BE PREPARED BY AN ATTORNEY AND REVIEWED BY ATTORNEYS FOR SELLER AND PURCHASER BEFORE SIGNING.

THIS INDENTURE, made the 25TH DAY OF JULY 2006

between **RACHEL O. LEWIS**
18 Pleasant Place, Brooklyn NY 11233
BROOKLYN, NEW YORK 1122·

X *R.O.L*

party of the first part, and **MARIE C. LAZAR**
2660 8TH AVENUE APT 15C
NEW YORK, NEW YORK 10030

party of the second part,

WITNESSETH, that the party of the first part, in consideration of Ten Dollars and No Cents ($10.00), lawful money of the United States, paid by the party of the second part, does hereby grant and release unto the party of the second part, the heirs or successors and assigns of the party of the second part forever,

ALL that certain plot, piece or parcel of land, with the buildings and improvements thereon erected, situate, lying and being in the

As particularly described in Schedule annexed hereto and made part hereof.

BEING AND INTENDED TO BE the same premises conveyed to *grantor /mortgagor in deed dated March 23, 2006 and recorded march 31, 2006 in CFRN# 2006000182051 in the office of the Kings County Clerk. Same property known as 18 Pleasant Place Bklyn NY 11233.*
TOGETHER with all right, title and interest, if any, of the party of the first part in and to any streets and roads abutting the above described premises to the center lines thereof,

TOGETHER with the appurtenances and all the estate and rights of the party of the first part in and to said premises,

TO HAVE AND TO HOLD the premises herein granted unto the party of the second part, the heirs or successors and assigns of the party of the second part forever.

AND the party of the first part, covenants that the party of the first part has not done or suffered anything whereby the said premises have been encumbered in any way whatever, except as aforesaid.

AND the party of the first part, in compliance with Section 13 of the Lien Law, covenants that the party of the first part will receive the consideration for this conveyance and will hold the right to receive such consideration as a trust fund to be applied first for the purpose of paying the cost of the improvement and will apply the same first to the payment of the cost of the improvement before using any part of the total of the same for any other purpose.

The word "party" shall be construed as if it read "parties" whenever the sense of this indenture so requires.

IN WITNESS WHEREOF, the party of the first part has duly executed this deed the day and year first above written.

Rachel Lewis
RACHEL O. LEWIS

IN PRESENCE OF:

202

LEONARD "SPAR" PERSON JR.

Acknowledgment by a Person Within New York State (RPL § 309-a)

STATE OF NEW YORK)

COUNTY OF *Kings*) ss.:

)

On the 25TH day of **JULY** , 2006 , before me, the undersigned, personally appeared **RACHEL O. LEWIS**, personally known to me or proved to me on the basis of satisfactory evidence to be the individual(s) whose name(s) is (are) subscribed to the within instrument and acknowledged to me that they executed the same in their capacity(ies), and that by their signature(s) on the instrument, the individual(s), or the person upon behalf of which the individual(s) acted, executed the instrument.

_____

(signature and office of individual taking acknowledgment)

VITTORIA GOMEZ
Notary Public, State of New York
No. 001GO6078395
Qualified in Kings County
Commission Exp July 29, 20 / 0

DEED

Title No.

RACHEL O. LEWIS
To
MARIE C. LAZAR

Section *6*
Block *15 68*
Lot *35*
County or Town
Street Address

Return By Mail To:

Marie C. Lazar
18 Pleasant Place
Bklyn NY 11233

Reserve This Space For Use Of Recording Office

203

LEONARD "SPAR" PERSON JR.

HEAVEN HOMES

777 KENT AVENUE BROOKLYN, NEW YORK 11205
TEL: 718-775-9086 / FAX: 877-233-0148

OFFER SHEET CLIENT NAME: Leonard Person Jr.

CLIENT ADDRESS: 5555 W. Dream Ave, Brooklyn, NY 11555

AGENT NAME: Rachel Lewis

PROPERTY ADDRESS: 55055 South Jefferson Lane, Brooklyn, NY 11555

COMPANY NAME: Heaven Homes, LLC
TEL NUMBER: 718-775-9086 FAX NUMBER: 877-233-0148

ATTORNEY: Abraham Hoschander
TEL: 718-555-5150 Fax: 718-555-5152

PRICE: $650K

DOWN PAYMENT: $10K to hold on contract

BANK: Cash Flow Funding, Inc.

LEONARD "SPAR" PERSON JR.

Date

Creditor Name
Creditor Address
City, State ZIP Code

RE: Your Name
Account #

To Whom It May Concern:
After careful review of my credit report, I have detected an error on my credit report regarding the account listed above.
This error was reported by your company:

QRS Credit Services, Account # 567890
Current credit report shows that I have a 30 day late payment in March 2007
My records show that I made a payment of $50 on March 3, 2007

I have provided (*names of the documentation*) which contains the error that I am disputing. I am requesting that you investigate this matter and make the necessary corrections to my account.

Please inform me in writing within 30 days to verify you have completed your investigation.

Sincerely,
(your signature)

Your Name
Your Address
City, State ZIP
Your Phone

LEONARD "SPAR" PERSON JR.

Thank You for your interest and purchase of my book. I hope this book was a benefit to you and I wish you much success and wealth on your journey in life. God Bless!

P.S. Remember, YOU are your greatest Asset and Liability in life, so before investing in anything else invest in YOURSELF!

In addition to that, don't ever be afraid to take risks. If it makes money then it makes sense. If you have nothing, then there's nothing to lose. Take that risk because THE GREATEST RISK IS NOT TO TAKE ONE AT ALL!

LEONARD "SPAR" PERSON JR.

NOTES

.